# Globalizing City

*Space, Place, and Society*
John Rennie Short, *Series Editor*

OTHER TITLES IN SPACE, PLACE, AND SOCIETY

*Alabaster Cities: Urban U.S. since 1950*
John Rennie Short

*The Boundless Self: Communication
in Physical and Virtual Spaces*
Paul C. Adams

*The Global Crisis in Foreign Aid*
Richard Grant and Jan Nijman, eds.

*Imagined Country: Environment, Culture, and Society*
John Rennie Short

*Inventing Black-on-Black Violence: Discourse,
Space, and Representation*
David Wilson

*Migrants to the Metropolis: The Rise
of Immigrant Gateway Cities*
Marie Price and Lisa Benton-Short, eds.

*The Politics of Landscapes in Singapore:
Constructions of "Nation"*
Lily Kong and Brenda S. A. Yeoh

*Tel Aviv: Mythography of a City*
Maoz Azaryahu

*Verandahs of Power: Colonialism and Space in Urban Africa*
Garth Andrew Myers

*Women, Religion, and Space: Global Perspectives
on Gender and Faith*
Karen M. Morin and Jeanne Kay Guelke, eds.

# Globalizing City

*The Urban and Economic
Transformation of Accra, Ghana*

# City

## *Richard Grant*

SYRACUSE UNIVERSITY PRESS

Copyright © 2009 by Syracuse University Press
Syracuse, New York 13244-5160

*All Rights Reserved*

First Edition 2009
09  10  11  12  13      6  5  4  3  2  1

The paper used in this publication meets the minimum requirements
of American National Standard for Information Sciences—Permanence
of Paper for Printed Library Materials, ANSI Z39.48–1984.∞™

For a listing of books published and distributed by Syracuse University Press,
visit our Web site at SyracuseUniversityPress.syr.edu.

ISBN-13: 978-0-8156-3172-9 (cloth)      ISBN-10: 0-8156-3172-3 (cloth)

**Library of Congress Cataloging-in-Publication Data**

Grant, Richard.
Globalizing city : the urban and economic transformation of Accra, Ghana /
Richard Grant. — 1st ed.
p. cm. — (Space, place, and society)
Includes bibliographical references and index.
ISBN 978-0-8156-3172-9 (cloth : alk. paper)
1. Urbanization—Ghana—Accra.  2. Accra (Ghana)—Economic conditions.
3. Globalization—Ghana—Accra.  I. Title.
HN832.A65G73 2008
307.7609667—dc22
2008046644

*Manufactured in the United States of America*

# Contents

# Figures

# Maps

# Tables

RICHARD GRANT is a professor in the Department of Geography and Regional Studies, University of Miami, Coral Gables, Florida. He is a human geographer with specializations in economic and urban geography. His research interests include economic globalization, globalizing cities, the work and economy of slums, and international and regional trade patterns. He has been conducting extensive fieldwork on urban and economic transformations in Accra, Ghana since 1995. His research has been funded by two National Science Foundation grants as well as the National Geographic Society. *Globalizing City* presents a theoretical argument based on empirical research that cities in Africa are not excluded and can be better understood as globalizing cities.

# Acknowledgments

I DID NOT KNOW WHAT TO EXPECT on my first trip to Accra in June 1995. I anticipated it would be an eventful trip but could never have anticipated that I would write a book on the city. My work in Accra had a suspect beginning. I arrived for my very first visit and my luggage did not make it until a week later. The taxi that I hired at the airport came to a sudden stop on pot-holed Cantonments road, half-way between the airport and Osu. The driver asked me to pay the fare at that point and I obliged as he scampered off to fill a container with petrol, assuring me he would return. He returned, and we continued onto my final destination, a cheap hotel in the commercial heart of the city.

So much has changed in Accra since 1995. The taxi service at the airport has been formalized (a large part of it anyway) and the drivers wear smarter blue uniforms and display (if requested) a printed sheet with official fares. The taxi vehicles have become more reliable and costly and even some now are air-conditioned. The roads and general infrastructure around the airport as well as the airport itself have been greatly improved. The cheap hotel has been rebuilt to a higher standard and is no longer inexpensive. Large facets of the city have been transformed and in the process, Accra no longer has the feel of a collection of villages, but now has a more metropolitan ambience. This urban transformation has brought new challenges as well as opportunities, and has resulted in complicated changes, some of them visible; most require unearthing.

In 2008, Accra is a globalizing city; Accra and other cities in Ghana hosted the Twenty-sixth African Cup of Nations soccer tournament in spring 2008 and the spectacle received global attention. So much that happens in Ghana, fifty-one years after independence, now is monitored both from afar and locally. Accra, in particular, as Ghana's globalizing node, is in a heightened process of transformation. My work is a serious attempt to document, analyze, and think about the ongoing urban transformation, particularly in light of the international arena becoming a more important driver.

I HAVE LEARNED MUCH about the city over the years. In this book, I draw together my various research efforts and writings, add to them, and connect the pieces in a framework that sheds light on the impacts of globalization processes on urban Accra. Some of the chapters in this book are based on working texts published at different stages in the advancement of the research. The original references are: chapter 2, R. Grant and J. Nijman. 2002. "Globalization and the Corporate Geography of Cities in the Less Developed World." *Annals of the Association of American Geographers* 92: 320–40; chapter 3, R. Grant. 2005. "The Emergence of Gated Communities in a West African Context: Evidence from Greater Accra, Ghana." *Urban Geography* 26: 661–83; chapter 4, R. Grant. 2007. "Geographies of Investment: How Do the Wealthy Build Houses in Ghana?" *Urban Forum* 18 (1) 31–59; and chapter 5, R. Grant. 2006 "Out of Place? Global Citizens in Local Spaces: A Study of the Informal Settlements in the Korle Lagoon Environs in Accra, Ghana." *Urban Forum* 17: 1–14.

I am grateful to many scholars, friends and institutions for their support of my work. I began conversations about Africa and Accra with Deborah Pellow, an anthropologist at Syracuse University over a decade ago when we shared offices next to each other in the Global Affairs Institute. John Mercer encouraged me to visit Accra to begin a new project. I am indebted to Paul Yankson, from the University of Ghana at Legon, for his numerous conversations and field excursions to various parts of the Accra and its environs over the years, and for his assistance and guidance in the survey research. Farouk Braimah of Peoples' Dialogue became a very good friend and is a tremendous source of information on many of the newer informal settlements that have emerged in Accra over the last decade or so. Richard Dornu-Nartey, former deputy minister of Lands and Forestry and current director of Land for Life, was very generous in providing background and historical insights on various urban issues. The African Studies Association annual conference provided an important intellectual environment to present my research and keep up with the latest research undertaken by the many Ghanaian geographers. Thanks to Ian Yeboah, Kobena Hanson, and Kwadwo Konadu-Agyemang (now only with us in spirit), and many others for their insights, criticisms, encouragement, and good humor. The National Science Foundation and the National Geographic Society were kind enough to support parts of research, and without their financial support this book would not have been possible. University of Miami students such as Lynsey Irwin, Daniela Belloli, and Kathleen Poncy provided help to various parts of the work.

MY THINKING ABOUT ACCRA in the global setting was greatly sharpened by conversations with colleagues Jan Nijman, Chris Rogerson, John O'Loughlin, Alan Mabin, Peter Muller, Peter Taylor, Marie Huchzermeyer, and others too numerous to mention. I greatly benefitted from conversations I had with colleagues of the Wits Housing Studies Group in Johannesburg when I was a visiting researcher there in fall 2005. John Rennie Short, the series editor of Space, Place, and Society at Syracuse University Press, was always encouraging of my Accra book project. Chris Hanson provided excellent cartographic expertise to this project. The reviewers of the book did a great job in helping me enliven the topic, as well as draw out my arguments.

My greatest gratitude is for my family. Adriana was always willing to listen to ideas as well as provide feedback. Adriana and Sofia accompanied me on a visit to Ghana in October 2005, and seeing Accra through their eyes was great fun and very refreshing for my work and writing. The book was supposed to be finished before Natalia arrived in November 2007. Her pending birth hastened my writing and help me move toward completion. No doubt like many authors before me, I have come to realize that infants have a way of growing faster than book projects. It is to Adriana, Sofia, and Natalia that I dedicate this work.

# Abbreviations

| | |
|---|---|
| ACS-BPS | Affiliated Computer Services-Business Processing Services |
| AMA | Accra Metropolitan Assembly |
| BP | British Petroleum |
| CBD | central business district |
| CBO | community based organization |
| CEPIL | Centre for Public Interest Law |
| COHRE | Centre on Housing Rights and Evictions |
| EPZ | export processing zone |
| FDI | foreign direct investment |
| GA | Greater Accra |
| GAMA | Greater Accra Metropolitan Assembly |
| GCG | Ghana Cyber Group |
| GFZD | Ghana Free Zones Board |
| GHI | Ghana Homes Incorporated |
| GHPF | Ghana Homeless Peoples Federation |
| GIPC | Ghana Investment Promotion Centre |
| GNIPC | gross national income per capita |
| GNPPC | gross national product per capita |
| GREDA | Ghana Real Estate Developers Association |
| GSE | Ghana Stock Exchange |
| GSS | Ghana Statistical Service |
| HABITAT | United Nations Centre for Human Settlements |
| HFC | Home Finance Corporation |
| HTA | Hometown Association |
| IGO | intergovernmental organization |
| IMF | International Monetary Fund |

| | |
|---|---|
| IRS | Internal Revenue Service |
| IT | information technology |
| JV | joint-venture |
| KLM | Royal Dutch Airlines |
| KLERP | Korle Lagoon Ecological Restoration Project |
| MIT | Massachusetts Institute of Technology |
| NGO | nongovernmental organization |
| NPP | New Patriotic Party |
| OECD | Organization for Economic Cooperation and Development |
| OPEC | Organization of the Petroleum Exporting Countries |
| PD | People's Dialogue on Human Settlements |
| RA | residential association |
| SAP | structural adjustment programs |
| SDI | Shack/Slum Dwellers International |
| UN | United Nations |
| UNCTAD | United Nations Conference for Trade and Development |
| UNDP | United Nations Development Programme |
| UNIDO | United Nations Industrial Development Organization |
| USAID | United States Agency for International Development |

# Globalizing City

# 1

# Introduction

*Globalizing City*

GHANA PARTICIPATED FOR THE FIRST TIME in the June 2006 World Cup Finals held in Germany. Ghana's debut was an important event in the country's history. "The Black Stars," as the team's supporters fondly refer to the national team, are professional soccer players employed by some of the world's elite clubs, such as Chelsea Football Club (United Kingdom), AS Roma (Italy), and Fernerbahce (Turkey). Accra native and Ghana's best-known player, Michael Essien, is Africa's most expensive footballer ever, following his transfer from Olympique Lyonnaise (France) to Chelsea in summer 2005 for US$45.87 million. In the German finals only one Ghanaian-based player, Shilla Illiasu, took to the field (Illiasu was a player for the Kumasi-based Asante Kotoko during the finals but has since been transferred to the Saturn Football Club, Russia).

What is striking (and similar to other African countries represented at the finals) is that virtually all of the regular team members ply their professional trade outside of their home states. Moreover, Ghana's first professional match after the German Finals (on August 15, 2006) was against neighboring Togo. Significantly this match was held not in Ghana, Togo, or even Africa but took place on European soil at Griffin Stadium in London. Professional soccer at the highest level is just one of the many indicators revealing the extent to which important national events are now routinely held outside national territory, how many high-profile Ghanaians operate as transnationals (keeping one foot in Ghana and one foot beyond), and the extent to which local and national revenues are connected to wider global flows of peoples and monies.

Many of the contemporary global-to-local and the local-to-global connections that are vital to Ghana are much less visible. For instance, the impact of the Ghanaian diaspora is much more difficult to quantify. We know that national policy promotes efforts facilitating Ghanaians in the diaspora to take an active role in the current development of Ghana, and we know that the more visible role of wealthy nonresidents in urban and economic development is indirectly encouraging future migration streams abroad, but it is difficult to put exact numbers on these phenomena. The volume of any type of international flow to Ghana (trade, investment, aid, etc.) does not stand out on global economic maps. The sum of all of these flows, however, is significant in the Ghanaian context, given a national population of 22.4 million in 2006. Moreover, foreign financial flows to Ghana appear to be delocalizing important aspects of Ghana's urban economies. For instance, in Accra niche property markets for gated enclaves for nonresident Ghanaians have been developed. The internationalization of Accra's urban economy has impacts in deep and unquantifiable ways: it alters people's horizons toward more (but sometimes less) engagement with the world beyond. More concretely, it is encouraging individuals to adapt, strategize, and network vis-à-vis Ghana in a wider world.

In this book, I explore the impacts of international dimensions of urban and economic change in Ghana's largest city, Accra. This exploration is based on eleven years of research on Accra, details the major global penetrations in the urban economy, and explores changing relationships among people and places in this context. The research entailed extensive fieldwork that included 652 corporate surveys, 300 household surveys and over 100 interviews with policy makers and key urban agents from real estate developers to slum-dweller organizations. It also draws on secondary data provided by national organizations in Ghana (e.g., the Ghana Statistical Service [GSS], the Ghana Investment Promotion Centre [GIPC], the Bank of Ghana). I asked myself three questions throughout my research. How has the international arena become a more powerful driving force in urban change? What are the most salient impacts of globalization on the spatiality of urban life? What are the most important impacts of the international arena on urban spatial development? The changing urban context is reflected across the range of the urban-economic spectrum. For instance, at both extremes of the urban spectrum, from elite gated community residents to the poorest of slum dwellers, city residents now think and act beyond the confines of the city and employ global strategies to mediate their positions in the contemporary city.

Accra is a very different city from the "typical" African city conceptualized primarily in local and regional terms in the earlier nationalist era. This more internationally oriented city represents an incomprehensible city to government policy makers and others who fail to grasp the extent of the transformation, and who instead still situate Accra in national, national-regional, and local terms. The closest parallel in terms of the city's exposure might be found in the colonial era and its urban spaces described in rich detail by scholars (e.g., King 1995; Myers 2003). In essence, this book is about looking out at the world from a prism centered on the real and lived experiences of Accra urbanites who are engaging the world beyond.

GREATER ACCRA: THE CASE STUDY CITY

Accra is an important city in the West African region, and is currently the capital city of Ghana. The rise of Accra as an urban center dates to 1877, when the colonial headquarters were relocated from Cape Coast. Accra was selected as a site for colonial administration for a number of reasons, prominent among them were health-related issues (building up a newer area was thought to protect Europeans from native-born diseases) as well as perceived locational advantages (a sheltered harbor and central location on the Gold Coast, close to the prime meridian) (Brand 1972a; Brand 1972b; Grant and Yankson 2003). A visitor to Accra in 1874 portrayed the area as "one compact mass of thatched buildings arranged in a haphazard manner and separated by narrow crooked streets" (Stanley 1874, 77) but this was to change dramatically in time.

Officially, "Greater Accra" refers to a broad administrative region (comprising GA, Accra Metropolitan Assembly [AMA], Tema, Dangme West, and Dangme East), but more commonly researchers conceptualize urban Accra as the built-up metropolis centering on AMA and fanning out into the adjacent areas of Tema and GA districts. Throughout this book I refer to Accra when discussing the built environment and the urbanized city per se. Urban Accra is bounded by the Gulf of Guinea in the south, by the

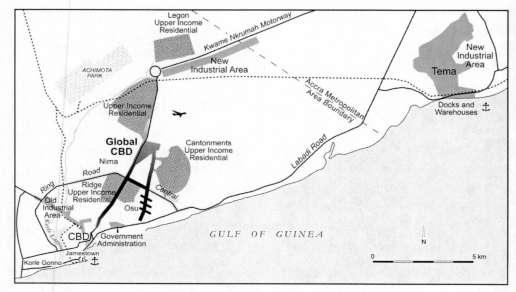

Map 1.1. Accra in a Globalizing Context. Source: Grant 2007.

University of Ghana in the north, by Tema Township in the east and Danso-man in the west. Beyond these areas the urban environment fans out in all directions in peri-urban sprawling development.

According to local population experts, Accra's official population in 2007 was 1,970,400, an appreciable increase of 311,463 since the 2000 census (GSS 2002), but the experts also acknowledge that it might be considerably higher (official census figures undercount slum dwellers, migrants, and regular sojourners).[1] Although Accra is not among the largest cities of the world, or even of Africa, its growth rate (among the fastest-growing metropolitan areas in West Africa) and the extent to which it is changing is significant. Annual population growth rates early in the twenty-first century hover around 4 percent (Habitat 2001, 300), and the city's spatial expansion has been spectacular.

To put this in perspective, over the last ten years or so "the number of urban residents has doubled, the areal size of the city has increased by over 300%" (Yeboah 2001, 68) and some 153,966 new houses have been built

1. Communication K.B. Danso-Manu, head of Data Processing, GSS, August 21, 2007.

(Yeboah 2003a, 114). Unlike other cities where administrative policies place limits on uncontrolled sprawl, Accra has experienced extensive growth and expansion, whereby city boundaries are pushing the urban frontier farther and farther away from the traditional urban core. Grant and Yankson (2003, 65) describe "the present city as stretching for about 30 kilometers from east to west, and about 12 kilometers from north to south," and most of this phenomenal urban expansion has proceeded since 1986. Within the built-up city itself there is considerable open space between Teshie and Tema, where large tracts of land are reserved for military use. All of this has been accomplished even though the gross national income per capita (GNIPC) had not moved beyond US$320 by 2003 and many urban residents survive on less than US$2 per day (World Bank 2005). One must ask: How has such extensive development been possible?

The "making of the town" of Accra (Parker 2000; Acquah 1957; Brand 1972a) and the historical and geographical development "from a fishing village to a millionaire city" (Konadu-Agyemang 2001b, 61) have been extensively detailed elsewhere. My work in this book builds upon this baseline, emphasizing the current international dimension in urbanization processes, a dimension that is likely to grow in influence unless major policy upheavals occur because of an unanticipated reversal in global orientation. The theme of this book is the making of Accra in the contemporary globalization era.

A contemporary globalization lens puts an emphasis on identifying globalization processes and individuals employing global strategies (Murray and Myers 2007). This lens also sheds light on international networks by explaining how links are maintained, guarded, adjusted, and reconfigured locally from Accra (Murray and Myers 2007). Obviously, not all urban residents participate in globalization, but all are affected by it "for better or worse" (Konadu-Agyemang 2000, 469; Gifford 2004). The urban impacts of globalization are highly differentiated locally, reflecting variations in global exposure, occupation, education, income, migration experience, family histories, networks and connections beyond, and so forth. Even though a growing proportion of Ghanaians have newly become urban residents, some city residents are not truly globalizing in the context of linking to the world beyond. Certainly there are many individuals living in Accra who have weak contacts to the global economy and who live locally rooted lives. Moreover, there are urban residents who emphasize a rural orientation to family and home villages, and who privilege these connections above all else in strategizing about their daily lives.

After twenty-four years of liberalization policies, however, most urbanites draw increasingly on material resources that span the globe. Most urban residents are pragmatists and cosmopolitans in this regard. Urbanites in Ghana have always been known to be resourceful, and many have connected beyond the local whenever possible, but the sheer scale of this trend is intensified in the contemporary era. Increasingly, urban residents seek to enlarge the spaces of their operation by jumping scales (whereby economic and political power established at one geographical scale can be combined with another, and typically there is a simultaneity of scales, whereby there are interflows

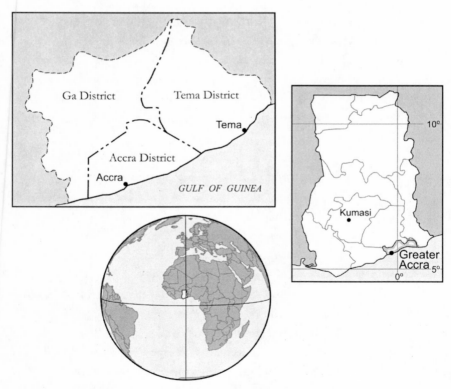

Map 1.2. Geography of Accra. Source: Grant 2002.

between the local community and the global environment and visa versa) so that local urban livelihoods are increasingly imbricated in a variety of global processes. Overall, the current globalization era adds another layer of complexity in that many urbanites have to operate simultaneously at a variety of scales (e.g., neighborhood, city, international).

The combining of global and local processes is producing a globalizing city: a production that is evolving and far from complete. The extent of the ongoing urban transformation is remarkable. As Simone (2004, 11) emphasizes, the transformation is "so extensive and deep as to have substantially displaced most functional centers of social gravity in both the countryside and city. . . . At the same time the city remains highly dynamic, a fertile incubator of new ideas, economies and social collaboration" (Simone 2004, 11). This urban environment is best described as truncated modernization: the evolving city is fragmented, chaotic, and spatially messy. It does not fit neat categories and/or simple compartmentalizations into traditional and modern, formal and informal. Moreover, the city has outgrown the clear spatial demarcations of the colonial era. The emerging urban and economic spatial formations are less than clear.

CONTEMPORARY GLOBALIZATION
AND URBAN DEVELOPMENT IN ACCRA

The information presented in this book contributes new knowledge about globalization based on extensive field research; its central argument: cities in Africa, like Accra, have *not* been left out of globalization. There is a widening, deepening, intensification and growing impact of global connections on the local economy and on local engagements with the world beyond. Globalization, in its embrace and impact, further divides the urban space and population as it integrates urban economies like Accra. As a consequence, the globalization era is associated with intensified uneven development in Ghana and in Accra, in particular. The best way we can spatially frame this uneven globalization is to situate it in the context of a hyper-differentiation of space (Grant and Nijman 2004). In essence, this is the spatial accompaniment of the hypermobility of capital. Hyper-differentiation comprises more than conventional definitions of uneven development; it involves both quantitative and qualitative transformations. It is expressed in increasing a divergence among places and individuals, taking place in the context of an ongoing reconfiguration and redivision of the global economy.

The urban impact of the globalization era can be best understood by framing it in historical context. Contemporary globalization represents the most recent of three historical episodes that changed the role and place of Accra in the global-political economy forever. Each of the historical episodes transformed the past, but the past is not obliterated. There is the persistence of continuities in the urban landscape, as well the creation of new spatial formations that may be separate and even competing. First, the decision by colonial policy makers to move the capital from Cape Coast to Accra in 1877 meant that the city became the administrative and commercial center; this elevated its importance and led to considerable expansion (Acquah 1957; Brand 1972a). During the colonial period, the city served as an entrepôt and gateway to the UK economy. Second, Ghana gained its independence in 1957, and Accra, as capital and leading city, served as a growth engine for the national economy. The postindependence period (1957–82) coincided with the nationalism era in Ghana's political economy. The government concentrated on accelerating modernization, and the main thrust of government policy was import substitution (Songsore 2003). Despite the rhetoric of balanced growth and even national development, the spatial structure of the colonial economy remained intact and new industrial and infrastructural improvement efforts in Accra complemented the colonial spatial organization of the city. The third historical episode and the foreground to this book is the government's decision to open up the economy in 1983 when a structural adjustment program was negotiated with the World Bank and the International Monetary Fund (IMF), and the state implemented a wide range of liberalization policies that, in turn, facilitated a deeper and wider engagement with the global economy.

In Accra, the impacts of globalization are widely recognized and debated, but research on the spatial effects of globalization has lagged behind; many of the changing spatialities of urban life have been theorized but are under researched. According to Murray (2004, 38) "the built environment is both a site and a source of social power: places are not only the material and symbolic embodiment of concealed power relations, they are the enabling devices that facilitate, structure and mediate norms of market-driven investment, production and consumption." The built environment, its shape, contours, and accessibility set limits on possibilities for the conduct of everyday life. Corporate offices, gated residential communities, export processing zones (EPZs), and slums, for example, are not merely in the background or simply benign; they carve out distinctive spaces and are part of the transformative process.

Central to understanding these new geographies of globalization is to emphasize the specification, location, and role of agency in the process. Instead of framing Accra as predominately marginal to the larger urbanizing world, it is more illuminating to conceptualize the city as a place of engagement and as a platform of mediation for local as well as global agents. Foreign investors, foreign property developers, nonresident individuals, and expatriates are leading participants in the transformation process. But they have also found willing local collaborators and forged important local-global ties, not just with government and the business community but also with individuals who, for better or worse, view their urban futures as more and more connected to the world beyond their known local communities.

THE THREE GLOBALIZING MOVEMENTS

There are three movements in which globalization becomes grounded in Accra. First, globalizing processes are ushered in from above. International organizations, the government, and its institutions aim to create a policy environment to harness global capital. The liberalization policy environment increases the transnational mobility of capital. In the Accra context, the city becomes a 'theater of accumulation' (Armstrong and McGee 1986) and circulation of capital, whereby foreign direct investment (FDI), new foreign companies, and international transfer of funds (remittances and savings of the diaspora now allowed under a financial liberalization regime) become ever more present. Above all else, the liberalization policy environment privileges the role of external actors and foreign capital in the local economy. The establishment of new agencies such as the GIPC and the Free Zones Board, and the centrality of these agencies within policy making are indicative of the new policy tilt. When foreign investments become grounded locally, they can form many local partnerships and arrangements that also rely on locals for support. For example, in the corporate environment they are often manifested in joint-venture (JV) business arrangements, and foreign companies can reach into the informal economy through subcontracting arrangements. Globalization from above, by its very momentum, triggers various reactions and a wide array of local adaptive strategies.

The second powerful movement involves locals harnessing a different type of global expertise and interacting with a different global environment (civil society as opposed to global capital). Most commonly in the literature, globalizing from below is usually conceptualized in terms of various forms of local resistance, such as grassroots activism. Some of the opposition to globalization from above focuses on broader economic forces (ethnic nationalism, anti-globalization protests, evangelical movements, etc.), but many efforts of globalization from below do not oppose global capitalism, rather seek to benefit from the new global context. Most saliently this has been expressed through marginalized individuals working in concert with nongovernmental organizations (NGOs) to change local urban policies and to demand a space in the local economy. Currently, interventions in housing for the urban poor do not have to be dependent on the World Bank and/or national governments (Huchzermeyer 2004). Some organized members of the poor are developing a capacity to learn and liaise with similar groups across national borders to formulate their own housing strategies and to reposition themselves within their local political context (Appadurai 2001). Slum-dwellers' organizations, working in concert with international NGOs and homeless people's federations in other locations (within country and outside of national territories), are a good example of an effort to install a globalization from below.

In a third movement, in-between globalizing occurs. This movement captures the adaptiveness of subjects that are neither entirely foreign nor entirely local. In many ways, in-between globalization has been facilitated by the fluidity of international migration and travel back and forth. Return migrants are a good example of how globalization proceeds in between. Potentially their networks are neither exclusively rooted in the initiatives of the immigrants themselves (i.e., from below) nor from above, dependent on institutional actors and external agents. Returnees operate in an in-between space and are often the missing and unknown agents. Based on their former experiences (having lived here, there, and here again), return migrants are able to combine traditional social networking and transnational networking. Many pursue transnational practices, and their lives revolve around linking different places and practices. According to Portes et al. (1999) it is the "intensity" and "regularity" of exchange that are novel among contemporary diasporas and that enable migrants to support and link development in a number of locations at the same time.

In this book, I explore the geographies of globalization within these three globalization movements. I posit that globalization is manifested in an uneven spatio-temporal development of capitalism (Grant and Nijman 2004). I take issues with world-city researchers who categorize African cities as "black holes" of marginalization and excluded or "excorporated" from the global economy (Short 2004a; 2004b). Instead, I present research evidence showing that globalization is ushered in from above, from below, and from in between simultaneously. Combined, these processes transform the urban economy in dramatic ways.

## ACCRA AS A GLOBALIZING CITY

The extensive world-city research literature has paid scant attention to cities in Africa. Outside of Johannesburg, full-fledged global cities in Africa do not exist. Van der Merwe (2004) emphasizes that sub-Saharan Africa is a huge information lacuna; African cities are often overlooked and portrayed as isolated and as lower down in the global urban hierarchy. By some criteria African cities may appear isolated (Simon 1992a), but it cannot be concluded that they are irrelevant to the global economy. At the other extreme, King (2004) proposes that all cities be considered as world-cities. This may be stretching the reality for most cities in Africa, considering that most states have not been fully liberalized. The reality for those cities leading in liberalization efforts (e.g., Accra, Gaborone) is likely to be somewhere in between. A more middle ground, argued by some scholars (e.g., Robinson 2006; Rogerson 2005) may be more on the mark. Robinson (2006, 538) emphasizes that when viewed from within these cities—"places allegedly off the global map"—the global economy is of enormous significance in shaping their fortunes and futures. In many ways, Accra, like the vast number of cities in the less developed world, is an "ordinary city" compared to the global cities of London, New York, Tokyo, and Paris.

This brings into focus an urgent need to better conceptualize and understand "ordinary cities" in terms of globalization (Robinson 2006). Many researchers have raised strong objections to world-city approaches that presume to ground urban theory in the experiences and histories of western cities (Robinson 2006; Grant and Nijman 2002). Furthermore, it is evident that the types of data used to study world-cities are not available for African cities (Simon 1992b). Even if they were, these data would not be as useful. The data limits in an a priori way the kinds of questions that can be legitimately addressed within the world-city framework (Murray 2004). It is also clear that different data are more relevant for studying non-world-cities. For instance, Taylor's (2001) research shows that the connectivity of NGOs in a world-city network is a better measure to capture the lower circuits of globalization than the networks of nonexistent branch offices of leading Fortune 500 companies. There is a consensus among researchers that local data collection is vital. Filling gaps in the data through local fieldwork by employing surveys, interviews, and other techniques is essential for understanding the cities of the world for which data are scarce. Such efforts are critical for grounding globalization and for yielding new insights into the workings of "ordinary cities" and for improving theorization of cities in the less developed world.

This is all the more urgent because earlier conceptualizations of African cities in the global economy—"the colonial city," "the African city," "the Third World City," and the "traditional city"—are now outdated. All of these were developed in isolation from each other, and none seem capable of explaining the present spatial imprint of globalization on African cities. We need an approach that is theoretically informed *and* based on primary research. In many ways, this means a return to the intensive fieldwork and primary data collection that characterized African urban research in the 1960s, but more important, the research needed now must be framed within the context of the changing global economy.

The framing of Accra in both the context of globalization and the context of Africa is complex because there is the double problematic of what exactly makes a city "African" as well as what are the unfolding global processes. The African city is a far broader and more culturally sensitive topic than I can explore in this book. My intention is neither to establish a geographical specificity nor to detail a particularly African modality of urbanization; instead I aim to link the African and global contexts. The impact of colonialism, the ensuing integration into the world economy, local idiosyncratic features, national development experiences, and the actions of local agents all account for differentiating African cities within a heterogeneous group. Furthermore, I contend that in the face of global economic restructuring, the ushering in of free market policies, increasing exposure to global and diaspora cultural inclinations, and similar forms of contemporary external engagements are eroding differences among African cities and, in general, among cities across the less developed world. This is not to deny the importance of African influences on family life, business practices, traditional sources of land and community attachment, and so forth. Instead, I contend that global pressures have resulted in more tensions, and in some instances, it is modifying traditional practices. For example, in the family domain, individuals in a globalizing city may tilt toward prioritizing nuclear as opposed to extended family units. In the business arena, enterprises may lean toward relying more on foreign capital than on local. In the housing environment, global knowledge about real estate products and trends may influence local housing tastes toward private, single-family dwelling units over traditional multifamily dwelling units.

In this book, I detail the city's new spatial arrangements that are the result of engaging in the globalization process. I employ the term "globalizing city" to conceptualize Accra in the context of globalization in cities in the less developed world. In the literature the term globalizing city has been employed to describe "other cities" in "other places" but vis-à-vis global cities (see, e.g., Oncu and Weyland 1997). I employ a globalizing city framework through an approach that examines the city from the center of its economic activities outwards. As such, I contend that globalizing cities are imbricated in the process of globalization, but their involvement in this process relates not to being either at the top or bottom of it, but rather to a particular context. I recognize the process is not uniform and that all globalizing cities are not converging toward a single model of a global city. However, there are grounds for asserting that globalizing cities are a discrete category of cities. Pacione (2005) alludes to some of the elements.

THE PRINCIPAL CHARACTERISTICS of globalizing cities are guided by a number of theoretical propositions:

1. A globalizing city is a city undergoing profound transformation in the way it is integrated into the global economy. It is a result of the introduction of extensive liberalization policies, but the reach of market forces is limited because of constraints on economic development and national economic growth. Opportunities are limited but not excluded by the widespread prevalence of an informal economy, remnants of nonliberal policy regimes (bureaucratic "red tape"), and traditional systems (e.g., landholding arrangements).

2. In the global-local nexus, globalizing forces become more powerful and their control more spatially extensive. Local forces are relatively weaker but also can be geographically extensive, and there are many instances of intermingling.

3. Globalization processes operate unevenly, bypassing certain places and peoples. Differences are accelerated by the speed at which capital can be deployed and by opportunities that individuals have to harness this capital, and there are multiple knock on effects throughout the urban area.

4. Globalizing forces are mediated by local and historically contingent forces as they penetrate from above, in between and below but come to ground in particular places.

5. Economic forces are the catalyst in the globalizing process, but there are important ramifications in the social and political arenas as well.

6. Globalizing cities can be distinguished from global cities in terms of the prevalence of small companies—especially of "bootstrap enterprises"—over larger companies, the bending and blending of formal and informal markets, informality in many arrangements (word of mouth, family involvement, labor relations, etc.), increasing circulations of migrants, and by the dearth of information about the functioning of the market (e.g., investments, profits, household budgets and finances, etc.); information that is generally public (in global cities).

7. Globalizing cities are urban environments where there are inherent tensions between global ways and local ways, resulting in multiple coexisting modernities in general, but at times colliding modernities can result.

8. Although globalizing cities are characterized by transformation, they may be in a permanent state of *becoming,* neither global nor traditional, but combining and integrating the two domains in evermore diverse and complex ways and never attaining the status of global city.

Presently, the impact of global processes on local urban change in globalizing cities is unclear (Simon 1992b). Researchers have established that these cities crowd out other cities in their region as they exhibit a "regional push" by serving as growth engines for their region in the global economy (Grant and Nijman 2004). Some of the details of globalizing tendencies in Accra have been researched by scholars (e.g., Pellow 2003; Hanson 2005; Yeboah 2003a), but Accra as a globalizing city has not been examined. The media sensationally report on the volume and extent of the role of foreign influences in Ghana, and particularly in Accra as the gateway city. Three examples of recent claims follow:

• *BBC-Online* reporter Briony Hale presents Accra as the answer to those "in search of Africa's Silicon Valley." (2003, 1).

• "Remittances to Ghana amounted to over US$4.5 billion in 2005, making it the largest foreign exchange earner," surpassing gold, cocoa, and manufacturing production (Ghanaweb 2006a, 1).

• *Time* reporter Ta-Nesisi Coates (2006, 1) discusses "investors landing with investment dollars and business skills . . . in the friendliest country in West Africa to do business."

Drawing on some of this evidence and on trends that have been identified by globalization researchers (Simon 1992a; Yeboah 2003a; Yeboah 2003b; Pellow 2002; Pellow 2003), I anticipate an important presence and role for FDI, a highly visible presence of foreign companies, a surge in producer services, the development of real estate markets, and more spatially mobile transnationals. Transnational networking involves connecting to sources of global capital and expertise beyond a country's borders and cementing new relationships in the process so that individuals operate simultaneously in the international and local domains. I also expect that new transnational networks play central roles and are different from the traditional extended Ghanaian family and village networks that have been well documented in the literature. It may be too early in the transformation process to determine if transnational networking has become as important as local networking, but it is fair to assume that they are being combined into the workings of a globalizing city.

## CONCLUSIONS

My chapters demonstrate that globalization is a complex process, involving interlocking sets of processes that are not reducible to a single trend or manifested in a single outcome. Globalizing outcomes are multiple and take various forms. Most obviously, globalizing processes delocalize the local economy, residential property, and land markets, and remake economic geographies by linking both nonresident Ghanaians and Accra residents with wider spaces of activity beyond.

With respect to the production of urban space, five key dimensions of globalization will be examined. In each of the main chapters of the book, I explore one of these key dimensions. In chapter 2, I examine foreign companies and corporate space followed by globalizing residential spaces and the spread of gated communities in chapter 3. I explore land sales and residential building boom in chapter 4 because globalizing from above and in between account for significant changes in residential geographies. In chapter 5, I consider the theme of in-between globalizing and the role of returnees and their networks and spaces. I then examine globalizing from below and the role of slum dwellers and slum-dweller organizations in transforming the city in chapter 6. Each of these five interwoven elements plays an important, albeit uneven, role in the development of globalizing spaces in Accra.

A central argument of this volume is that the globalization debate is not nearly as global as it ought to be. There is currently a gross imbalance in the geography of knowledge production, where most urban research and publications remain overwhelmingly concentrated on Europe and North America and on places that decreasingly represent the world of the twenty-first century (Mabin 2001, 183). Potentially both undemocratic as well as misguided, much existing theorization on world-cities may be "depriving urban theory, planning and policy making in the North of ideas . . . and . . . insights of the dynamic urban experiences of diverse regions of the world" (Harrison 2006, 320).

The globalizing city framework is presented to reassert and reemphasize the role of many ordinary cities in Africa and in the less developed world in terms of the urban consequences of contemporary globalization processes. In particular, I emphasize the emerging urban and economic geographies within a globalizing city. In the process of elucidating the spatiality of a globalizing city, many important questions are examined: How is it that individuals buy property when traditional land law does not permit land sales? How can individuals pay between US$25,000 and $300,000 for houses when Ghana's per capita income is around US$400 and mortgages are scarce? How is it that there are almost 2,000 foreign companies registered with the government when globalization theorists assume that Accra is not yet on the world economic map? What kinds of business (large and small) prosper in this environment? On what kinds of networks do entrepreneurs rely? What is the role of transnationals in the process of transformation?

Research on globalizing cities is still in its infancy. Data collection and field research is difficult and time consuming. By outlining some of the complex urban and economic geographies that exist within transnational space I make a preliminary start. In the concluding section I draw together a set of observations and discuss the policy environment and globalizing cities in the context of urban studies. The conclusions raise many new questions. There is still much work to be undertaken on globalizing cities, and I hope this work will stimulate more theoretical and empirical research on various aspects of this genre of cities.

# 2

# Globalizing from Above

*Foreign Companies and Corporate Spaces*

GHANA, AND MORE PARTICULARLY ACCRA, does not come to mind when thinking about investment hot spots globally. For example, UNCTAD's *World Investment Report of 2005* lists Ghana as an "underperforming country" ranking Ghana in eightieth place out of 140 countries in the world in terms investment flows. However, World Bank regional rankings on "Doing Business in 2006" bring Ghana more into focus: Ghana is ranked first in West Africa for doing business and overall seventh in Africa (GIPC 2006, 2).

The research literature on world-city networks posits that Africa is marginal to the global economy (Van de Merwe 2004). However, world-city observations (and many others) about globalization and cities in Africa are not grounded empirically from the bottom up, and instead are based on thin evidence that relies on incomplete data. As such, there are too many stereotypes and misinterpretations about globalization and urban Africa. For example, the notion of foreign companies that predominates in the world-city and globalization debate is partial (based largely on the largest companies from the Organization of Economic Cooperation and Development [OECD]), and thus *excludes* everything else. It is well known that many of the companies that become established in Africa are small enterprises often investing as little as US$10,000 to begin with. The only way we can uncover these companies is by local field research.

To correct this oversight, in this chapter I focus on identifying foreign companies and their role in transforming the urban economy of Accra. The concentration on foreign companies is justified because they are major agents of globalization with a highly visible presence. The focus on foreign compa-nies also involves a closer examination of FDI flows; combined they are the best indicators of the globalization from above phenomenon. My research sheds some light on the volume of flows but also discuss the type of engage-ment. The type of engagement will be assessed by revealing the extent to which investors' pursue wholly owned companies as a market entry strat-egy or whether they embed themselves with local partners and pursue JV arrangements. My efforts concentrate on examining foreign companies from the ground upward, based on fieldwork I conducted in Accra, which resulted in datasets on foreign and domestic corporations, and I extrapolate the most current trends, using the most recent GIPC data.

To capture the extent of the current changes in the transformation of the urban economy, I situate Accra's urban development within its historical context. I outline the four historical phases in urbanism that led to the emer-gence of the contemporary city: precolonial, colonial, national, and global. I argue that, during each of these phases, urban geographies have changed in relation to the role of the city in the global-political economy. Subse-quently, I analyze different geographies of corporate activities and consider the apparent connections between the foreign and domestic corporate sec-tors. In the concluding section, I return to a discussion of the liberalization policy environment and consider what policy efforts are needed to improve the functioning as well as integration of the corporate sectors.

## THE INTEGRATION OF ACCRA INTO THE GLOBAL ECONOMY WITHIN THE HISTORICAL CONTEXT

The distinction between precolonial, colonial, national and global phases is based on the nature of the global-political economy's organization. It is a distinction that highlights a city's external connections (facilitated or con-strained by domestic factors) to the global economy as key to its internal spatial development. In this section, I first detail the development of Accra and its mode of integration into the global economy emphasizing the two most recent historical phases. I then draw connections between the intensity of integration into the wider global-political economy and the most salient effects on the city's economic geography.

*The Mode of Integration*

*Precolonial*: Most local experts equate the establishment of Accra with the development of a coastal fishing village in the late sixteenth century (Gough and Yankson 1997, 9). The earliest known settlers on the stretch of coastline now named Accra were the Kpesi people. Ga-speaking migrants from "Niger country" reached this area in the sixteenth century, and they made their homes among the Kpesi and absorbed them into their communities (Acquah 1957, 16). During the precolonial period in West Africa the main urban settlements were largely inland, where they functioned as desert ports along the southern termini of the trans-Saharan trade in gold, slaves, salt, and forest products (Gugler and Flanagan 1978, 6). European accounts of this period refer to the numerous ports on the littoral and to the "great towns" in the interior of the country that contained "multitudes of people" and were "richer in goods and gold than the coastal towns "(Kea 1982, 23).

*Colonial*: The colonial period is best categorized by two episodes. In the first, from the fifteenth to mid–seventeenth centuries, most contact between European traders and West Africans occurred in coastal settlements. The slave trade reinforced this development of coastal trade centers, where warehouses and permanent installations were needed to accommodate commodities and people drawn from the interior. During this time, a number of forts were built in what is known as present-day Accra (Fort Ussher by the Dutch in 1605, Christiansborg Castle by the Swedes in 1657, and Fort James by the British in 1673). However, a Portuguese map of the seventeenth century indicates that Accra was not connected to any of the major trade routes along the Gold Coast (Kea 1982, 31). Moreover, Accra was largely outside the wider urban spatial system, which was centered on Kumasi in the interior of the country (Campbell 1994).

The second episode during the colonial period involved the British consolidation of power on the Gold Coast in 1874, when they defeated the Ashantis. The rise of Accra as an urban center dates to 1877, when the colonial headquarters were relocated there from Cape Coast (Acquah 1957). Accra was chosen as the site of the colonial administration for a number of reasons, prominent among them were health issues (specifically securing the health of the European residents) as well as geographical and strategic concerns (Accra was the geographical center of gravity for the UK colony and located near the prime meridian, which runs through present-day Tema). Moreover, the earthquake of 1862, which had severely destroyed large portions of Accra, presented colonial rulers with an important opportunity to plan, rebuild, and reorganize the space. Its selection as the seat of government, though, ran contrary to the pattern in most other West Africa countries. For instance, Abidjan and Dakar were chosen as capitals because of preexisting economic advantages, but Accra was selected largely based on initial noncommercial advantages.

WITH THE ARRIVAL of the colonial machinery came a large number of merchants, and in the process, political and economic power became focused on Accra for the first time. It became linked to the United Kingdom as a gateway city and expanded in size and population as a direct result. The integration of Accra into the external economy reversed the traditional urban and economic patterns of development in Ghana by anchoring the economy to a coastal location. The major terminal point of the colonial system was Accra, and transport links pushed directly inland by the early 1920s to sources of exportable commodities. The cocoa boom in that decade deepened the interdependence of Accra with the external economy, and at the same time most external investment became concentrated in a single resource and sector. Once cocoa grew to preeminence among Accra's exports, commerce replaced government as the primary element in the urban-economic base. Over one-half of all firms in Accra were engaged in cocoa trade by 1930 (Brand 1972a, 105). Accra continued to develop as a warehouse city rather than a factory city throughout the rest of the colonial period.

*National:* From 1957 until 1982 Accra was shaped by nationalist economic policies. The Nkrumah government promoted the capital city as a growth pole for the national economy, and successive administrations all prioritized building up the infrastructure of Accra in national development planning (AMA 1999). Specific policy measures aimed for a Ghanaization of industries. For instance, the Ghanaian Business (Promotion) Act of 1970 permitted Ghanaian monopolies for small firms engaging in import-export trade, for some manufacturing, such as cement production, and for a variety of service industries, such as taxis, printing, and advertising (Killick 1978). Moreover, the government starved the foreign sector of imported raw materials, spare parts, and equipment through tariffs and import licensing arrangements. The combination of these various policy measures limited the exposure to the international economy. Indeed many foreign companies had decided to curtail their activities in Ghana by the early 1980s (e.g., American Firestone pulled out of Ghana in 1984) (Dzorgbo 1998, 223). Instead the government dominated the economy, functioning as the major shareholder in over 400 different enterprises in the financial, manufacturing, extractive, and agricultural sectors (Grayson 1979; World Bank 1994).

*Global*: The global phase was initiated with the introduction of liberalization policies in 1983. Market reform involved full adoption of the World Bank's and IMF structural adjustment policies to halt the economic decline that had begun in the 1970s. Specific policy measures were implemented to attract foreign companies by eliminating barriers to foreign direct investment, upgrading the physical infrastructure, privatizing state-owned enterprises, establishing export processing zones (EPZs), and reducing barriers to trade. For instance, over 100 state-owned enterprises were privatized in Ghana (Mmieh and Owusu-Frimpong 2004). The net impact of this range of liberalization policies was to increase the exposure to the global economy. Global exposure was also enhanced by the establishment of the Ghana Stock Exchange in 1989, which was slowly able to expand the number of company listings (particularly foreign listings) so that twenty-nine companies have been listed by 2006. GIPC also devised attractive campaigns to harness Asian investment and the investments of nonresident Ghanaians (the latter was facilitated by holding a Homecoming Summit in 2001). All of these efforts amounted to what President Kufuor has called "The Golden Age of Business for Ghana" (GIPC 2006, 1).

Over the years, the government has expanded the reach of investment efforts to include after-care initiatives. For instance, the government facilitates an In-Country Investors' Outreach Program for periodic consultations with a specific country's investor groups to discuss solutions to problems facing foreign investors. For example, in March 2006 GIPC and the Indian investor community in Ghana held a meeting to discuss and remedy some obstacles to conducting business in Ghana. Moreover, the government had formed working partnerships with a variety of international organizations to market investment projects to foreign investors. For example, the government advertises new and existing local projects seeking an overseas investment partner with the United Nations Industrial Development Organization (UNIDO) (UNIDO 2003).

The main thrust of government's investment policies is to promote Accra as a gateway city serving as a connecting node with the global economy. The Gateway Project aims to enhance Ghana's competitiveness and Accra's position as a West African hub for import, export, storage, assembly, distribution, and transshipment of goods, services, and passengers (UNCTAD 2002). The project targets neighboring land locked and smaller economies to patronize Accra's port and airport facilities. A loan of US$50 million was provided by the World Bank to upgrade port and airport infrastructure (Grant and Yankson 2003).

*The Internal Spatial Organization of the City*

The mode of integration into the global economy has implications for Accra's internal economic geography. I turn now to sketching the main features of the city's economic geography in each of the phases.

*Precolonial*: The first coastal settlement was just to the east of Korle Lagoon, called the "fish village" (Acquah 1957, 16). It appears this original settlement expanded to encompass the oldest adjoining parts of present-day Accra; namely, Jamestown and Ussher Town. There is not a great deal of information about the spatial organization of Accra at this time. Archeological evidence suggests that the village was spatially organized around the sheltered harbors (Kea 1982) with "low-density shelters adjoining the coastline in an unplanned fashion" (Hubbard 1925, 21).

*Colonial*: Three European forts situated within three miles of each other formed a nucleus for foreign commercial enterprise in the early colonial period. In the shadows of the forts were walled Ga villages partially oriented to trading with the European merchants. Scattered settlements connected by footpaths rather than an urban clustered center characterized the emerging organization of Accra. Europeans lived in the forts, which additionally served as places for holding both slaves and commodities (Kea 1982).

During the nineteenth century, the role of the forts changed; they became centers of administration, housing government officials, troops, and later police. When this occurred, European traders began to locate outside of the forts, and the township of Accra was established. With the arrival of the seat of government in 1877, the British attempted explicitly to improve sanitation and living conditions in the area. As they had been for a long time, foreign and domestic sector distinctions were paramount. However, in the colonial phase the spatial organization of the urban economy was formalized. There developed a sharp contrast between the large foreign companies dominating the extractive industries and the relatively small manufacturing sector on the one hand, and the small-scale enterprises of indigenous groups or recent immigrants (e.g., Lebanese in Accra) on the other hand (Brand 1972a). European commercial and residential areas were clearly separated from native commercial and residential areas. A schematic representation of the spatial organization of Accra (similar to other colonial port cities) during the colonial period is shown in Map 2.1.

There were four main features of colonial Accra. First, the city was spatially organized around the port that functioned as a central node in the trade network between its hinterland and England. The city became the strategic center linking rail lines and shipping routes. The docks, warehouses, and railway terminals all supported the functions of trade, storage, and distribution. The port area was particularly important in terms of command-and-control, and functioned as a strategic bridgehead for the British government. Most of the buildings of the colonial administration and military bases were located in the immediate vicinity. Slum clearing took place, and the British attempted to superimpose rectangular-style patterns as a morphological variation on the existing unplanned city (Brand 1972a).

Second, adjacent to the port area was a well-defined European central business district (CBD) that functioned as the designated location for foreign companies. Most economic activities in this European commercial area involved trade, distribution, transport, banking, and insurance. Zoning and building codes were strictly enforced to maintain an orderly European character and atmosphere in the district.

Third, traditional markets or bazaars were located in a business district in "Native Town." This area comprised a mix of commercial and residential land uses. Much of its commercial activity involved trade of agricultural produce and crafts, small-scale industry, and retailing. The colonial government

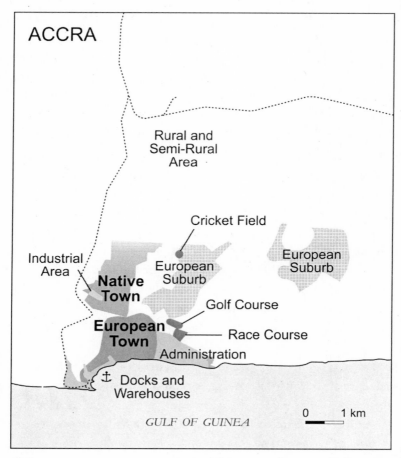

Map 2.1. Schematic Representation of the Economic Geographies of Accra During the Colonial Phase. Source: Grant and Nijman 2002, 325.

paid relatively little attention to urban planning in Native Town, which tended to exhibit congestion, poor structures, and unsanitary health conditions. The area was inhabited by natives and recent rural immigrants. Most important, the European town and Native Town were physically separated by a designed barrier: an open green area.

Fourth, a rigid policy of segregation ensured clearly demarcated zones for European residences near Accra's commercial center (e.g., Victoriaborg) or retreats further away on higher elevations (e.g., Cantonments).

With its luxurious homes, race course, golf course, polo and cricket field, tennis courts, and racially segregated hospital, "Victoriaborg was like a piece of England grafted into the townscape of Accra" (MacDonald 1898, 199–200). In sum, the colonial landscape of Accra exhibited a high level of segregation of foreign and native commercial and residential activities, with its economic geography displaying a significant degree of functional specialization and concentration (Brand 1972b). As participation in the international economy increased in the early twentieth century, and as population pressure built up, the boundaries between the different areas gradually blurred.

*National*: Transformations in the spatial organization of Accra occurred in the wake of independence (Acquah 1957; Brand 1972a). Apart from rapid overall population growth in Accra, resulting in significant geographical expansion, the spatial configuration was altered in four main ways. First, the foreign corporate and residential presence declined in relative terms. Elimination of legislation that had formerly discouraged native enterprises led to a rapid growth in the number of domestic companies, which were now free to locate around the city.

Second, the former European CBD was at once de-Europeanized and nationalized, both politically and economically. Administrative and military functions in the area were taken over by the national government. New large domestic companies favored a location in this area, leading to a steadily growing corporate density and a large number of domestically controlled companies. In addition, the area was nationalized in a symbolic sense with the location of a newly established central bank and state-controlled companies.

Third, the former native CBD (Native Town) became even more characterized by small-scale businesses, as larger companies moved to the emerging national CBD (the former European CBD). As a result of massive rural-urban migration in the postindependence years, the density and congestion in Native Town kept increasing. The rise of a national entrepreneurial middle class meant an explicit foreign urban space was diluted because income became the more important criterion for determining commercial and residential patterns. By the early 1980s, there was only a modest foreign presence in the urban economy of Accra.

## THE ECONOMIC GEOGRAPHY OF ACCRA
## AS A GLOBALIZING CITY

The liberalization era in Ghana has gone hand-in-hand with rapid rates of urbanization and expansion of the built-up area. However, urbanization proceeded in neither a planned nor an ordered way. In many ways the traditional landholding systems provided a check on emerging land use patterns. Much of the land is either vested in various stools and families with customary tenure. Government acquires land for public uses but even this can be fraught with complications and land can remain idle for many years. As a result of the traditional and state land systems that prevail in Accra, there is a shortage of land available for commercial use, and the real estate market began responding to this trend only in the late 1990s. Commercial real estate became available in pockets and at different times, resulting in a patchwork of corporate activities without government directed clustering. The only area that was an exception in terms of commercial available land was Tema; it represents an exclave of sorts, geographically separated from the city of Accra by a zone of open space but gradually more connected to the urban Accra. Tema became more linked to Accra after the development of its port in 1962, when Accra harbor was abandoned in favor of Tema's deeper and more sheltered harbor. Since then, an industrial area, warehouse and storage facilities, and extensive housing for workers have been built in the immediate Tema area.

The particular landholding systems, combined with the floodgates of globalization from above, have resulted in Accra's economic geography becoming more dispersed over the years, and in the decades since the mid-eighties. The suburbanization of economic activity, especially manufacturing, in that same time period has centered on Tema and the Light Industrial area. Small concentrations of export-oriented industries have emerged in export processing zones (EPZs), the most built up of which is the Light Industrial area.

*Foreign Corporate Activity in a Globalizing City*

The most recent GIPC data (2007, 8) show that 2,129 companies have been registered in Ghana. The establishment of new foreign companies accelerated to unprecedented levels in the liberalization period: over 90 percent of all foreign companies currently active have been established since 1983. A surge in the establishment of new foreign companies coincided with the transition to democratic government in the 1990s. Over US$2.8 billion had been invested by foreign companies. FDI projects have created more than 73,000 jobs: 94 percent of these employ Ghanaians and 6 percent non-Ghanaians (Mmieh and Owusu-Frimpong 2004, 591). According to UNCTAD (2002, 16) foreign firms also accounted for 75 percent of the increase in export earnings.

As already noted, the liberal investment climate offers a variety of options for foreign companies to enter the market. Foreign companies can establish 1. a wholly owned foreign company with 100 percent foreign equity, 2. a JV arrangement with a local firm/investor(s) or 3. a liaison arrangement (either as a full liaison office or by a lesser liaison commitment, such as securing a mining license). Although a firm's decision on how to enter an economy is based on complex internal company decisions (e.g., risk, opportunity, company strategy, etc.), local factors such as available land, government enticements, and the securing of local partnerships are increasingly important in determining the entry mode of FDI projects, especially in countries that are enacting liberalization policies.

Most foreign companies enter the Ghana market by a JV. Almost half of all foreign companies who establish their headquarters in Accra companies maintain a JV relationship. Thirty-seven percent of companies function as wholly owned foreign companies, and the remainder operate as liaisons. Most liaisons maintain a representative in Accra, which can be taken to indicate an interest in researching the marketplace for possible future investment opportunities. These preferences for JV arrangements continue the process by which foreign companies have been encouraged to participate in the economy. Prior to liberalization, national policy measures aimed explicitly to avoid dependence on wholly owned foreign companies. From the early 1970s, the government warmed to JVs with foreign partners for some Ghanaian holding companies in an effort to obtain financial support and secure more efficient management (Grayson 1979).

Unless there are some subtle ways the GIPC is steering investors into JVs, it appears investors have concluded that it is advantageous to forge local partnerships in Ghana. Such partnerships can provide foreign investors with several advantages, including country knowledge and experience as well as political suaveness. The lower initial investment requirement of US$10,000 to establish a JV, as opposed to the US$50,000 requirement to establish a wholly owned foreign company, may be important in explaining part of this trend as well. The prevalence of JVs indicates not only that globalization is not solely reliant on external capital but also that local strategic business alliances are an important consequence of liberalization policies.

The geographical origins of foreign companies in Accra reveal that liberalization policies have entailed opportunities for investors from across the world. Foreign companies from most countries of the world participated in businesses in Accra. Some of the largest companies have had a presence since the colonial era, when most FDI in Ghana originated from the United Kingdom. Firms such as Unilever, Cadbury, British Petroleum (BP), Standard and Charter, and Barclay's Bank have operated in Ghana since the colonial era. The sources of FDI have varied since the introduction of liberalization policies (Table 2.1). Traditionally, the United Kingdom was the largest source of FDI into Ghana, mainly into the banking and mining sectors, but now ranks third behind India and China.

TABLE 2.1

ORIGINS OF TOP TEN MOST ACTIVE FOREIGN COUNTRIES
IN CORPORATE ACTIVITIES IN ACCRA, 1994–2006

| Country | Total number of companies | Rank |
| --- | --- | --- |
| India | 217 | 1 |
| China | 212 | 2 |
| United Kingdom | 198 | 3 |
| Lebanon | 170 | 4 |
| United States | 133 | 5 |
| Germany | 115 | 6 |
| Netherlands | 73 | 7 |
| South Korea | 71 | 8 |
| Italy | 66 | 9 |
| Nigeria | 59 | 10 |

*Source:* Grant 1999; GIPC 2007.

In the 1990s, many companies from the developing world (particularly from China, South Korea, Nigeria, and South Africa) have also become active in Ghana. Chinese investments have flowed into infrastructure, trade, and minerals. Companies from India and Lebanon have been returning to Ghana, reviving early twentieth-century links when many Indian and Lebanese firms forged a major presence in the wholesale and retail trade sector and largely ceded the manufacturing sector to European firms (Garlick 1960). The presence of Asian investors in Ghana is the result of the GIPC's investment promotion programs. Malaysian companies, in particular (ranked twenty-third in terms of the number of companies), have become very active in the telecommunications sector—in television and films as well as in the provision of services for free trade zones. For example, a national television station, "TV3," as well as the film group, GAMA, are both Malaysian controlled, and Telecom Malaysia owns a 30 percent share in Ghana Telecom. Within the process of liberalization the government has become an active participant in the private sector and is forming new private sector partnerships, establishing itself as a minor partner. For instance, the Ghanaian government, international development agencies and a Malaysian company are developing an area in Tema as the first private free zone in Africa. However, the authorities of the Tema Free Zone have found it difficult to attract firms in large numbers and to foster clusters. Operators cite large parcels of idle land. Interviews with free zone officials reveal that only 15 to 25 percent of land is currently being used.[1] This considerable unused land gives a bad impression to new investors thinking of establishing companies in Accra and it also means that companies are likely to seek more established areas to locate their companies.

## Geographies of Foreign and Domestic Corporate Activities

The general geography of foreign and domestic corporate activities in Accra is illustrated in Map 2.2. First, Ussher Town is the traditional CBD and corresponds rather closely to the old European town in colonial times. It is the most densely concentrated area in terms of corporate activities, containing many high-rise buildings in close proximity to the ministries, and the

1. Interview with Andy Appiah-Kubi, deputy executive secretary, Free Zones, June 8, 2004.

Ghana Stock Exchange is located in the area. It contains the second highest concentration of Ghanaian-controlled companies of any business district in Accra and a small number of foreign companies, many of which were among the first foreign companies to be established in Ghana.

Second, the area labeled "Central Accra" includes Adabraka, Tudu, and Asylum Down. Corresponding to the old Native Town from the colonial era, it contains Makola Market, the largest market in the city, the most crowded commercial area in the city, and the focus of most commuter trips within the city. The bustling market spills over onto the walkways and roadways and leads to acute congestion. The overall area has a mix of corporate and residential functions, a visible presence of firms of Lebanese and Syrian descent, and a maze of side streets and back alleys. This business district has the largest share of Accra's domestic companies, though generally of small size. The number of foreign companies in this district is also small except for a cluster of foreign airline offices in its center.

The newest, and arguably most prominent, business district in Accra in the early twenty-first century is an area that stretches from Osu along Cantonments Road to the airport. It also covers the Ringway Estate and Ridge Area. The entire area is not commercial but foreign corporate activities are concentrated in a ribbon fashion along the main thoroughfares. Much of this area was initially used for residential purposes, but since the introduction of

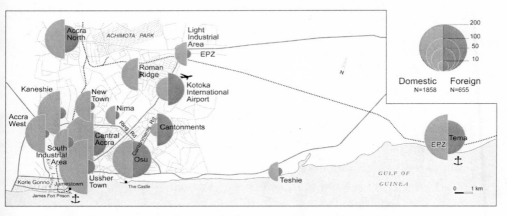

Map 2.2. Geographic Distribution of All Corporate Activity in Accra in 1999. Source: Grant and Nijman 2002, 328.

liberalization policies, properties along the main roadways have been rede-
veloped for commercial purposes. The area has modern low-rise buildings
with off-street parking, and stands in sharp contrast with the colonial archi-
tecture of Ussher Town and the bazaar atmosphere of Central Accra.

*Foreign Companies in the Services Sector*

FDI into Ghana has traditionally been in the mining sector. However, the
recent trend shows that the fastest growing sectors of the economy for foreign company involvement are in services (producer services: management
consulting, internet providers, and mobile phone providers; financial services: banks, investment brokers, and real estate services). By 2006, almost
one-quarter of all foreign companies participated in the services sector. Mining is still the largest sector in terms of the numbers of foreign companies,
and the privatization of mining after 1996 has aided this trend. However,
many mining companies are tiny and seldom move beyond the initial stages
of exploration, thus inflating the real number of active mining companies.
Recent falling gold prices have been taking their toll on the number of foreign companies engaging in mining (*Financial Times* 1999, 3), but rebound-
ing gold prices have renewed FDI in mining.

Foreign companies in finance and producer services are found in the
districts of Osu, Cantonments and the airport area (Map 2.3). The heavily
trafficked area along Cantonments Road in Osu (locally known as "Oxford
Street") is the focal point for most foreign producer services companies. New
paved roads, hotels, shops, and restaurants have increased the attractiveness
of the area for engaging in face-to-face business, an important aspect of producer services businesses. In the airport area a large number of these firms
cater to mining companies concentrated there (Grant 2001) and provide the
kinds of services that rely heavily on airport facilities (e.g., courier firms).

The producer services functions are in a formative stage in Accra. The
vast majority of producer services companies are small operations, and many
of the business and communication centers that specifically target businesses
also have to take on consumer clients in order to turn a profit. Moreover,
the locational choices available to newly arriving foreign companies within
Accra are limited. For national security reasons, property developers have

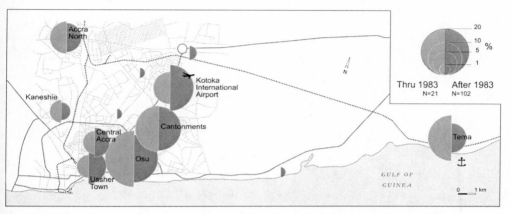

Map 2.3. Geographic Distribution of Foreign Companies in Finance and Producer Services in Accra in 1999. Source: Grant and Nijman 2002, 332.

been prevented from developing the only nearby vacant area, adjacent to the Castle, and recently arrived foreign companies have located further away from the existing business districts. Still, they are less than a half hour away from the old center (except during rush hours).

There are many examples of firms who based their headquarters in Accra to serve a regional market, in effect spearheading the Gateway strategy. For example, in 2001 the Ghana Post Company and TNT Express, a Dutch company involved in mail, express, and logistics services signed a JV to operate an international mail handling center for the West African region using Royal Dutch Airlines' (KLM's) cargo and facilities. Under the agreement an international hub and spokes system was established at Kotoka International Airport. The agreement not only allows for Accra to become a hub for international exchange of mails and parcels between the subregion and the world, but it also allowed for a lowering of air conveyance dues between Europe and Ghana.

Since 2000, outsourcing companies have also located in Accra. One of the largest players, ACS-BPS (Ghana), employs more than 1,800 workers and is the largest information technology (IT) services employer in Ghana (providing support services in the healthcare, insurance, and transportation industries). To date, most of the outsourcing companies are U.S. companies who have moved parts of outsourcing operations to Accra. There are incidences of Ghanaian workers being coached to speak in American accents for call center work. Some of these companies are also contracted to do U.S. Federal Government work. For instance, Data Management International, a U.S. firm, processes environmental fines for the City of New York and is contracted by New York's Department of Environmental Protection. Since 2005, high-level discussions have taken place to establish a Ghana Technology Park to serve as a center where outsourcing companies can be concentrated. To date US$10 million has been raised by the Ghana Cyber Group (GCG), a technology company operating in information and communication technology space (Ghana Cyber Group 2006). GCG has taken the lead in putting together a consortium that involves the University of Science and Technology at Kumasi, Colombia University (United States), and the Massachusetts Institute of Technology (MIT, United States) to create and build the infrastructure needed. The proposed site is located within the Accra-Tema EPZ.

*A Contrast: The Geography of Domestic Corporate Activity*

To better appreciate the distinct spatial patterns of foreign corporate activity, it is useful to provide a contrast. The location of domestically owned import and export businesses is shown in Map 2.4. This kind of economic activity is internationally oriented, but it is small-scale, controlled locally, and of older vintage.

There is a long tradition of relatively small trading companies in Accra, dating back to the colonial period. The nucleus of import-export firms has been in the Native Town since the 1920s, when petty traders started to offer narrow lines of locally, nationally, and internationally traded goods. Europeans were disinterested in participating in these activities that produced little income beyond subsistence living. Many firms were originally owned by immigrants, particularly Lebanese and Syrian. During the national phase, legislation was introduced to reserve businesses for Ghanaians, inducing these one-time immigrants to become naturalized Ghanaian citizens. Thus, their firms have since been classified as domestic companies.

Domestic firms have few links to foreign companies (other than using their services, equipment and/or products). Research also indicates that Ghanaian domestic companies have smaller business networks than foreign companies in Ghana (even for similar sized companies in the same sector).

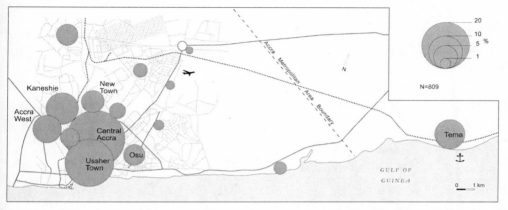

Map 2.4. Geographic Distribution of Domestic Companies in the Import-Export Sector in Accra in 1999. Source: Grant and Nijman 2002, 335.

Barr (1995) argues that domestic firms are far more likely to rely on familiar agents rather than to develop new contacts. No doubt this reflects that many of these companies were operational in the nationalist period where reliance on government and existing structures and organization was the norm. Barr (1995) describes domestic company owners as small isolated groups with few economic ties outside their locales and virtually no direct contact with larger businesses, government, or institutional programs and little knowledge of the market beyond Ghana. My interviews with domestic companies reveal similar evidence. Many domestic company interviewees expressed "abandonment" as a consequence of government policies that emphasize foreign investors and offer little to small domestic companies in the way of training, support, and involvement (e.g., international trade missions, etc.). There was an acute awareness that the government spends time in after-care efforts with foreign investors but does little in the way of offering services to assist in export promotion in terms of improving access to credit and loans that could allow domestic companies to cooperate and/or compete with foreign companies. As one interviewee put it "it pays to be a foreigner or to have a foreign partner when dealing with the government of Ghana."[2]

2. Interview with domestic business owner "Charles" who wished to remain anonymous, June 12, 2004.

*The Tripartite Organization of Specialized Business Districts*

The most significant change in the organization of corporate activities in Accra is the emergence of different CBDs. The lack of any planning in terms of land use and functions for the commercial heart of Accra (particularly manifested in the shortage of corporate office space and the citywide growth of microenterprises) has meant market forces have become more salient in determining land use. Presently, three CBDs are discernable and represent the main clusters of corporate headquarter activities in Accra. A response to the geographical agglomeration of many of Ghana's economic activities in Accra, these CBDs—Osu/Cantonments and Airport, Ussher Town and Central Accra—are all different in terms of historical origin, economic activity, and most important, relevance for foreign and domestic companies.

Interviews with company directors revealed few linkages among the specialized zones and particularly between the foreign and domestic corporate sector. One foreign corporate sector interviewee put it "we have a global horizon compared to a local. We work with locals but engage them within our organization and as such, they learn to become more global in the process. Overall, much of the local corporate sector is too informal and small-scale to foster linkages with."[3] A domestic corporate sector interviewee said "we have links with local firms but none with foreign firms in Ghana. We don't know if we could benefit from linkages to the foreign corporate sector. We possibly could. Our government talks about the potential linkages with big companies but none have materialized. Unless you have connections to government, then you stay in your own local environment with your local connections and have limited contacts with the business world beyond."[4]

Central Accra overlaps in large part with the old Native Town from colonial times (Map 2.5). It has residential functions and a mix of small

3. Interview with Emmanuel Idun, commercial director, Unilever Ghana Limited, June 12, 2004.

4. Interview with domestic business owner "Brenda" who wished to remain anonymous, June 12, 2004.

domestic trade, craft, and retailing businesses; there is a noticeable absence of foreign companies. Central Accra also contains the Makola Market, the largest market in Accra for petty trade, in spite of the government's efforts to decentralize market functions by its promotion of Kaneshi Market. Most

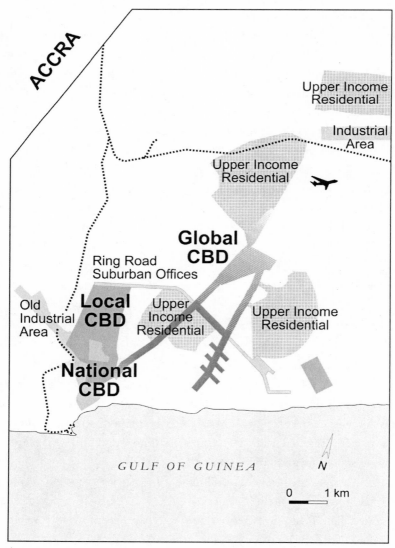

Map 2.5. Schematic Representation of the Economic Geographies of Accra During the Global Phase. Source: Grant and Nijman 2002, 338.

businesses are locally oriented within the metropolitan area, and the area functions as a *local* CBD. Ussher Town corresponds closely with the European CBD from colonial times. The district's residential function is limited, and it contains many large domestic companies and a substantial number of foreign companies, many of which are older established companies in Accra (e.g., Cadbury and Barclays). Most businesses have a pronounced orientation to the economy of the country as a whole, so the area functions as a *national* CBD. Finally, Osu/Cantonments and Airport are relatively newly developed business areas. As previously mentioned, this district has a large concentration of foreign mining, finance, and producer services, and functions as a *global* CBD. Osu along Cantonments Road is quite distinctive within the district because a prominent up-market commercial strip has emerged along this major thoroughfare. The rising urban middle class and the cosmopolitan elite can be found shopping and dining in this area. In contrast, the vast majority of Cantonments and Airport areas are residential with commercial clusters of new buildings along the major roads and converted residential office space within the neighborhoods. Businesses in this area, more so than in any other district, are articulated with the global economy. The overall success of these new CBDs and their abilities to develop complementarities will be vital to the success and future development of the Accra metropolis.

## FUTURE POLICY AND ACCRA'S CORPORATE GEOGRAPHIES

Globalizing from above has resulted in powerful new imprints on the urban economy. The liberalization era is comparable to the colonial phase in terms of the clearly visible spatial articulation of external linkages in the urban economy (compare Map 2.5 with Map 2.1). The main difference in the contemporary period is that market forces rather than colonial spatial planning are driving spatial formations (Grant and Short 2002).

The most significant recent development in the corporate geography of Accra is the formation of three distinctive CBDs. The further development of these may help promote synergies among businesses in each specific district. It may also alleviate some pressures on the traditional CBD, which suffers from acute traffic congestion. The development and promotion of three distinct corporate identities for the three CBDs may bring some order to the currently fragmented economic geography of the city. Beyond the three CBDs, businesses locate in a disorganized and fragmented manner.

However, the development of corporate sectors only represents a small portion of all Accra business activities. The formal sector is relatively small. Much more prominent today (outside of the CBDs) are home-based, microenterprises. Low-level services and production activities, such as chop bars (local fast-food operations), kiosks (corner stores), cement block manufactures, and building material retailers, are the norm along major roads. Often these noncorporate economic activities are involved in fueling the further expansion of Accra's frontiers. The further development of microenterprises development, unless it is held in check, could hinder existing as well as future FDI. Clearly, investors are interested in a city that both functions efficiently and has good aesthetics.

One of the most pressing policy challenges is to embark on comprehensive land use planning. To date most planning has been based on the outdated Town and Country Ordinance of 1945, which does not provide for connections between land use planning and policies for social and economic development. Comprehensive land use plans have not been implemented in the liberalization era. Planning since 1983 has centered on initiatives to attract FDI and has been more infrastructure oriented and sector based to the detriment of spatial planning (Ofori 2002). The Strategic Plan for the Greater Accra Area, developed in the early 1990s (UNDP and HABITAT 1992) with assistance from the World Bank, has not been implemented (except for the Ring Road and industrial development components). Clearly, there is a need for more spatial planning and spatial concentration. It is clear that the free zones need to be reconsidered. The Light Industrial area and the Tema zones need to be converted into multifacility economic zones. These and other zones should be transformed into industrial parks that offer investors immediate project start-up and cluster firms inside the zones.

There are also broader policy challenges raised by the contemporary corporate geography of Accra. In the current liberalization climate, the government has put its hopes on laissez-faire development strategies that strengthen regional clusters of economic activity. The notion of "regional push" connotes the role of regional engines of growth in the wider economy (Scott 2002). In Ghana and many other African countries, the geographic agglomeration of economic activities is now primarily based in the large urban centers that serve as drivers of the national economy. This unbalanced economic development raises some important challenges: Can the Accra economy and its specialized CBDs drive the entire national economy? Can unbalanced and unplanned urban development in Accra be sustained in the long run?

The evidence is mixed about the extent of positive linkages and spillovers from the foreign corporate sector into the domestic corporate sector. In terms of establishment and market penetration, the most salient aspect of the FDI environment is that most FDI investors enter the Ghanaian market in JV arrangements whereby the foreign partner typically contributes the largest share of capital, access to credit, and know-how (e.g., product improvement, training, management methods, etc.), and the local partner contributes local and regional market knowledge (e.g., contacts, knowledge of government regulations, local customs, etc.). However, the minimum capital requirements for establishing a foreign investment in Ghana are low by global standards. Raising the minimum capital requirements would improve the quality of investments and allow for more focus on larger investors who can offer wider linkages.

Many of the largest foreign companies, listed on the Ghana Stock Exchange [e.g., Unilever (Ghana), Guinness (Ghana), Mobil Oil (Ghana), Standard Chartered Bank (Ghana)], have benefitted the global profile of the Accra corporate environment and developed a wide array of local linkages. Evidence of direct links among smaller foreign firms (particularly those with modest start-up capital) is much less apparent. A United Nations survey (2003, 86) found evidence of "building trust" among the foreign and domestic sectors but little else. Many foreign firms in residential building, financial services, and auto repairs are developing multiple linkages with domestic firms. Other sectors such as mining and tourism are characterized by foreign and domestic firms operating in separate spheres with few links to each other.

Two sets of weaknesses exist concerning the FDI environment in Ghana. There are factors beyond the control of the government: concerns about spillovers from conflicts in the region, global concerns about terrorism, a lack of clarity about China's economic engagement with Ghana (as well as the rest of Africa), efforts to keep investments at home, the fickle nature of

FDI into markets classified as developing/emerging, the small size of the domestic economy, and national economies within Accra's gateway region. In addition, there are weaknesses that relate to prevailing local conditions: low levels of economic development and infrastructural development (compared to rival investment locations e.g., Johannesburg), the peculiar local land acquisition problem, the limited and only recent experience with investors, the poorly organized employment market, stemming the migration of skilled workers abroad, and limited successes in training and development of a global workforce. Most pressing seems to be land reforms to ensure that investors can lay claim to their property within a legal framework. The GIPC is still in the process of creating a registration of lands and a GIPC Land Bank for investors.

The government has promoted FDI without properly reinforcing the potential contributions of the domestic corporate sector. The small size of the domestic corporate sector and large number of small firms makes it very difficult to build successful clusters. Without a strong domestic business sector to act as partner, supplier, and/or customer, it is hard to realize FDI potential. The government needs to direct more attention to create a hospitable environment for domestic start-ups that could serve as suppliers of goods and services for foreign companies. Policy attention should be directed toward helping local entrepreneurs to become regionally active in Ghana as well as in other regional markets. Most important, the GIPC needs to refocus on establishing outward investment services to complement and counterbalance existing inward orientated investment services. The investment reform process needs to begin with a rewrite of some of the investment legislation, now more than a decade old, and domestic organizations need to be involved in the process.

# 3

# Globalizing Residential Spaces

*The Spread of Gated Communities*

GATED COMMUNITIES HAVE BECOME a striking feature of contemporary urbanism. Gated communities have been defined as "privately governed residential areas with restrictive entrances in which, normally, public spaces have been privatized. . . . They include new developments and old reconverted areas, they exist in cities and suburbs, in wealthy and poor neighborhoods" (Blakely and Snyder 1997, 2). In a much cited study, Blakely and Snyder (1997) estimated that up to 9 million U.S. residents live in 20,000 proprietary residential communities bounded by walls and entrance gates, and that the trend has increased since this estimation. More recently, research has confirmed that it is not just a U.S. phenomenon; this form of residence has also greatly expanded in cities in Argentina, Brazil, South Africa, Saudi Arabia, Lebanon, China, etc. (Donaldson and Lochner 2002; Landman 2004; Webster et al. 2002; Coy and Pohler 2002).

To date, their emergence in Accra has not been studied. The presence and extent of gated communities is an important marker of a particular form and order of residential development. Gated communities are foreign-inspired communities based on international architectural designs. Private enclave living is a clear spatial demarcation of globalizing spaces in the urban environment. These areas are physically separated and clearly demarcated in the residential environment; furthermore they clearly delimit property behind the walls and gates. The gated community phenomenon appears to represent a counter-response to the spread of informalization in land and housing that characterizes much of the residential building in Accra. Locally, gated communities represent a complete break from the past: a movement away from traditional conceptions of land and dwelling units, a preference for a different type of community, and a product that can be place-marketed, packaged, and sold to upper-income individuals and expatriates.

The development of gated communities in Accra is the latest and most salient episode in the transformation that is taking place in urban land markets. The change commenced with the introduction of liberalization policies in 1983. Prior to the 1990s, government legislation was unhelpful to private developers (Konadu-Agyemang 2001b; Tipple and Willis 1992), most land developed for residential purposes originated from the traditional land system, and transactions in this system created considerable impediments to developers interested in private residential project development (Quarcoo-pome 1992; Kasanga et al. 1996; Odame-Larbi 1996).

The liberalization era has also radically transformed property markets by the globalization of finance and the restructuring of FDI. The lowering of barriers to FDI in land, the development of vastly improved sources on residential projects (e.g., Web sites, brochures), and international lending and mortgage programs have all transformed the local real estate markets. Parts of the Accra real estate market now operate within an international real estate industry that facilitates the purchase of properties by wealthy individuals, many of whom make their living outside of Ghana. According to Mueller and Ziering (1992) real estate represents between 20 and 60 percent of the world's wealth, and its share of wealth is rapidly spiking in globalizing cities where property is integrated into the international market, often for the first time in the country's history. Property prices in Accra's gated communities are reasonably priced by international standards (but not by local). The influx of foreign funds into Accra residential developments has resulted in a marriage of local development processes and FDI.

Portions of the Accra's residential real estate participated in the global real estate boom of the last decade. How and why parts of the Accra residential environment became globalized can be understood only by a transnationalism lens. Transnationalism researchers (Waldinger and Fitzgerald 2004; King 2004) have shown that in recent migrations streams many migrants have been able to settle in a new country, and at the same time maintain close contacts with their place of origin. Transmigrants draw on commodities and objects from different habitats of meaning to create global culture "here" and "there" (Hannerz 1996; Pellow 2003). Their lifestyles and housing tastes are greatly affected (Okonkwo 1999); for instance, popular housing styles and residential models in migrant receiving countries can gain a global currency. We do not have reliable figures on how many Ghanaians live abroad: estimates suggest 3 million (Anarfi et al. 2003) and that 30 percent of all highly educated Ghanaians live abroad the *Economist* 2002, 38–40). A select portion of nonresident Ghanaians participate as transnationals and are having a major impact on Ghanaian economy and society. They remit huge sums of money into the national economy, particularly into sectors such as housing (Yeboah 2003a) and appear to be shaping preferences for private housing away from traditional housing. In the process, they participate in reimagining the world at home from afar and create spaces of global cultures inside the local urban arena (King 2004). Assessing the extent of the gated community phenomenon in Accra illustrates some of the changing housing aspirations and appeals of gated living, and sheds light on broader dynamics of urban, social, and economic transnationalism.

## GATED COMMUNITIES AS A COUNTER-RESPONSE TO INFORMALIZATION OF LAND AND RESIDENTIAL BUILDINGS

Within the last two decades, Accra has gone through far-reaching social and economic change, resulting in an increasing fragmentation of urban residential space. Extensive urbanization occurred because the city had a strong appeal to poorer sections of the rural population, whose hopes for survival lay in the diverse employment opportunities of Ghana's largest city or in its growing informal economy. Concurrently, investors and private sector professionals witnessed increasing opportunities as the city became engaged with the global economy. Foreign companies, international organizations, and NGOs became more involved in projects headquartered in Accra (Grant 2001), requiring housing for their workers. At the same time, transnationals also desired housing for their investments.

As emphasized, private sector residential development is a recent phenomenon. Mostly residential development undertaken in Accra is through individual builders rather than private developer companies. Land and housing is highly informalized whereby most individuals erect their own houses following a complex informal process involving all aspects of land acquisition, finance, and construction management outside of planning regulations. Costs are kept to a minimum but incremental building can take 15 years or more to complete (Odame-Larbi 1996; Antwi and Adams 2003a; Antwi and Adams 2003b). Most new residential units were built in unserviced areas and without uniformity of structures, plot sizes, or building standards (Konadu-Agyemang 2001b). This informal land market is characterized by widespread disputes in Accra: between 15,000 and 60,000 land-law cases resulted (Agbosu 2003). Private gated communities have emerged on the housing scene as a counter-response to the many land and building problems in the informal market.

Because of the newness of the gated community phenomenon in Accra, we know very little about the owners, occupants, and housing aspirations. Concepts like "the Ghanaian-family home," and "rent-free accommodation," central to earlier housing studies research (Korboe 1992), may not be useful for understanding the contemporary situation. In earlier times, homes served as a public good and entailed significant obligations and attachments. Korboe (1992, 1159) estimates that 25 percent of the population lived rent-free (blood relatives gain the right and in-laws the privilege of living free). Even those who decided not to live in the Ghanaian-family home maintained an inalienable right to the property for social functions. As early as 1990, a perceived stigma was attached to the Ghanaian-family home by individuals who were economically upward mobile. In many cases, living in the Ghanaian-family home represented economic failure (Korboe 1992, 1169). Prosperous individuals were often unwilling to remain in the family residence and to assume all the financial liabilities. The growth and spread of private houses in suburban locations (Pellow 2003; Hanson 2004) clearly complicates existing conceptions of homes, families, entitlements, and obligations, and raises the issue of whether the trend toward gating private housing communities is coupled with a trend toward reconceptualizing families toward more nuclear units. Housing associations have clear and fixed rules about how many occupants can live in the house, and the practicalities of living within a gated community also entail rules about who can enter and under what conditions, and who can use residential community services, etc.

The participation of private property developers in the Accra gated residential market signaled a major break with former traditions and practices. Real estate marketing and advertising strategies were engineered based on North American and European markets to attract potential buyers and sell units in Accra's gated developments. Glossy brochures, Web sites, targeted advertisements, and mailings were all employed to create a new housing industry standard. Most of the projects also kept selling in-house to avoid "quack" and unlicensed real estate agents who dominated the informal residential market. Branding was used to differentiate the products of different developers. The larger implications of a globalizing real estate niche are: this land became commodified, homes became commodified, and residential land values became driven by market values within these communities. More important, the profit interest of real estate developers determined the kinds of residential projects that emerged. Private housing was so expensive to construct in Accra because "70% of capital allocation for housing development goes into the initial development of the land and the provision of services and utilities" (Maloney 2004, 16). The best way to recoup significant outlay investments was to concentrate on the upper end of the residential market and to develop niche products like gated enclaves. Gated communities were targeted at individuals who could afford to pay premium prices for well-serviced residential projects: 1. exclusive individuals in Ghana, 2. transnationals (who wished to avoid building through informal channels, such as having to deputize the building to a relative, friend, or business associate, or to manage the building from abroad),[1] and 3. foreigners who desired comfortable living in a well-serviced and exclusive project.

SELLING PLACES: ADVERTISING AND MARKETING

The development of a real estate sector with a variety of real estate products is among the most important driving forces of residential change in Accra. Figure 3.1 illustrates the annual trends of private sector residential developments in the city based on an analysis of all real estate advertisements that appeared in Ghana's three largest daily newspapers. Although

1. Interview with William Opare, executive director, GREDA, July 12, 2003.

few advertisements were printed before 1990, the number of advertisements placed by private developers increased after 1991, coinciding with the increased number of large property developers entering the market (e.g., Regimanuel Gray). Private advertisements have registered a sharp and sustained increase particularly since the late 1990s. The number of gated community advertisements shows a steady increase, although it does not keep pace with the total number of advertisements from private developers. Nevertheless, gated community advertisements account for 20 percent of total private sector advertisements in 2003, confirming the establishment of a market niche.

The advertisement of gated communities peaks annually between June and August (Fig. 3.2), which corresponds to the holiday seasons in Ghana, when emigrants return for various activities. The marketing and advertising of gated developments occurs not only within the city, but more important, outside of the country. Property developers target wealthy emigrants by strategically placing advertisements in magazines like *Ghana Airways* (its in-flight magazine), *African Millionaire*, and *World Diplomat*. Interviews with property developers Trasacco Valley and ACP Estates confirmed the targeting of *African Millionaire* for marketing during the nonbusy

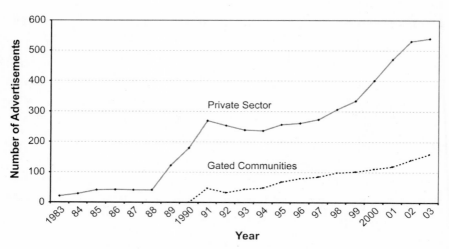

Figure 3.1. Private Sector Real Estate Advertisements. Sources: *Daily Graphic* 1983–2003; *Mirror* 1983–2003; *Ghanaian Times* 1983–2003.

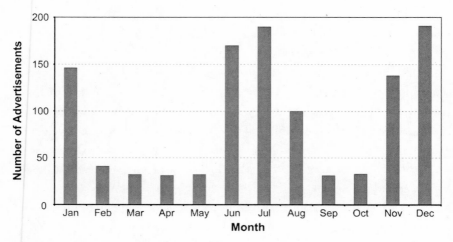

Figure 3.2. Monthly Fluctuations in Gated Community Advertisements. Sources: *Daily Graphic* 1983–2003; *Mirror* 1983–2003; *Ghanaian Times* 1983–2003.

Ghana travel seasons.[2] Moreover, private developers regularly participate in GREDA housing exhibitions abroad (e.g., London in 2005, Toronto in 2003, London, and New York in 2002, London in 2001) to market a variety of private development schemes to Ghanaians and real estate investors abroad. Usually, these programs are coordinated with targeted mailings to particular groups (e.g., Ghana-Chicago Club, graduate listings from the Accra elite, secondary schools).

The marketing of gated developments in Accra points to a globalizing local real estate industry. It is clear that private developers have employed the gated enclave model to mobilize offshore capital. Time and again, private developers emphasized to me in interviews that "everything with an expensive, international flair is selling in Accra."[3] Nearly all of the large private developers maintain comprehensive Web sites (typically house prices are updated on a monthly basis), and these sites offer online home purchase applications. A growing number of commercial real estate Web sites

2. Interview with Eddie Nartey, sales manager, ACP Estates, February 12, 2004, and Ian Morris, project manager, Trasacco Valley, February 14, 2004.

3. Interviews with estate developers and managers, February 10–16, 2004.

from Ghana (e.g., www.ghanacityguide.com) and from the United States (e.g., www.realestate.escapeartist.com) also regularly list houses for sale in Accra. Most of the large property developers have selling agents in North America and Europe to facilitate home purchase from abroad. GREDA also maintains a news bulletin online with success stories of home purchases from New York, London and Accra (Ghana Estates 2004). *Ghana Real Estates Magazine International* was launched in the United Kingdom as well as the Netherlands in 2004 to sell properties and to provide information about properties and real estate agents in Ghana. The magazine routinely advertises agents with offices abroad and in Ghana. For instance, Regalon International is an estate company with a presence in both London and Accra. Its slogan is "Live your dream. We will make your [Ghana] housing problems disappear." (*Ghana Real Estates Magazine International* 2004a, 65).

The demand for houses by those living abroad has been high enough to create opportunities for specialized firms, such as Ghana Homes Incorporated (GHI), an Internet-based company from the Bronx in New York, to provide consultancy services to prospective buyers. Among client services, they liaise with private developers and the HFC and provide an after-home purchase service by "verifying the existence, location, condition of the exact home purchase" (GHI 2004, 1). GHI's portal also features advertising banners from gated community developments in Accra (e.g., ACP Estates, Royal Palms, Lagoon View Estates, Vista Valley). Promoting the company's services, its directors note: "As expatriates ourselves, we can identify your needs and aspirations. We speak your language and know how to help you meet your needs and special requirements in home purchase."

Private developers' advertising and promotional literature emphasize a number of themes and provide clues of self-made images. The literature is also informative about the spread of enclave communities and about the culture of the market for these new products. One theme is prestige, also emphasized in advertisements of other world locations. Building designs with imported materials and developers with experience abroad are routinely highlighted. Most residential developments refer to "dream homes" and "exclusive designs." Estate management companies are highlighted for their professional management skills to assure that the property is maintained at a high standard. Community is another broad theme, also consistent with the global trend: "residential community," "quality lifestyles," and "good neighborliness" are frequently mentioned. A third theme—privacy and seclusion—is heavily promoted. For example, Royal Palms enclave boasts "a private estate set in delightful seclusion . . . one of the most valuable sites in Accra . . . a luxurious retreat for gracious private living." A fourth theme involves the security and safety concerns in Accra, which are very different from those in other cities. Security is emphasized in a planning sense of "secured land," "hassle free investments," and "planning order," "without all the previous difficulties and frustrations" that characterized housing acquisition in the 1980s. Overall, the physical security theme seems to be far less prominent for Accra gated communities' advertising than it is elsewhere. There are few mentions of walls, gates, or barriers, although maps depict these features.

Crime does not appear to be a significant factor for explaining the communities' development in Accra. For instance, the most recent Interpol crime statistics show 5.4 burglaries per 100,000 persons in Ghana, compared with 76.9 per 100,000 in Kenya, and Ghana ranks nineteenth of fewest burglary occurrences globally (Interpol 2004). Figure 3.3 shows the number of breaking and entering crimes in Accra between 1980 and 2001. Property offenses register a steady but modest increase, but nothing like the rate in Johannesburg, Rio de Janeiro, and Nairobi. In Accra, crime levels as indicated by various crime data have not increased substantially over the last twenty years, especially when one considers the urban expansion that has taken place. There were some spikes in the number of burglaries (two in the mid-1990s), but the trend declined by 1998 and has remained more stable since. Appiahene-Gyamfi (2003, 19) notes that burglary is almost ubiquitous in Accra and affects all groups, classes, suburbs, and neighborhoods. Nevertheless, the media reported a crime wave in 2002 and drew much attention to a small number of armed residential robberies, blaming organized criminals from Nigeria, Liberia, and Sierra Leone. In this context, the number of private security firms has grown: private security personnel dramatically increased to 50,000 personnel (*Africa Online* 2001; *Daily Graphic* 2003). Overall, perceptions of crime seem to be more important than real increasing crime in fueling the push toward gated communities.

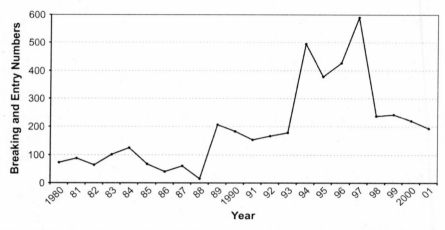

Figure 3.3. Breaking and Entering Crimes in Greater Accra, 1980–2001. Source: Ghana Police Headquarters 1980–2001.

## THE GEOGRAPHY OF GATED COMMUNITIES IN ACCRA

Although still a small portion of total residential housing in Accra, gated communities are becoming more salient. As of June 2004, twenty-three gated communities (15 to 600 units) are at varying stages of development. Most of the residential gated developments consist of houses. Four are exclusively apartment complexes. Individual units, depending on the residential development, range from US$30,000 to US$460,000. When all of the projects offering houses and apartments for sale are eventually finalized, they will provide 3,644 units (3,572 houses and 72 apartments). In terms of the overall housing stock, this represents less than a 3 percent contribution to given present numbers, but it nonetheless indicates the increasing diversity in the housing market, particularly at the upper end economically.

This investment in gated community projects amounts to US$434.8 million (at 2005 values). Such a sum would cover all of the costs for building more than 17,300 middle-class houses at Accra's average construction prices in 2005 and a considerably greater number of lower-income houses. To put the sum in perspective, it is equivalent to the country's total FDI for 1999–2003 (GIPC 2004b) and more than equivalent to Ghana's total cocoa exports (the largest commodity export). The discrepancy between house prices in gated communities and local salaries further supports the contention that Accra has one of the worst house price-to-income ratios among developing countries (Malpezzi and Mayo 1997). This discrepancy explains why expatriates are the main buyers of these houses. Expatriates find these houses to be competitively priced given their salaries and the sums of monies needed to enter the United States and/or European property markets. In comparison, expatriate dollars and euros buy a lot more house and accompanying amenities in Accra than cedis do. Nonresident Ghanaians are also heavily drawn toward the international designs, housing models, and amenities offered in gated community developments. Their housing tastes deviate from compound houses and extended family accommodations toward single-family units in private, secured, and well-serviced communities. Buying into a gated development offers nonresident Ghanaians a foot in both worlds but on their own terms. As a design director at a prominent gated development put it,

> Expatriates can have an American-style house with world-class amenities run by a local company with international experience away from but close enough to the African city. Most importantly, gated community residents get to choose when, and on what terms, they wish to leave their ordered estates and venture out into other places.[4]

Moreover, in addition to my catalog of larger gated communities (Table 3.1), smaller gated developments of fewer than eight houses were discerned. Smaller gated communities are generally built exclusively for rental and targeted to international organizations. Cross Creek Court in Cantonments is a good example of a six-house compound rented to the U.S. Embassy for its staff. There are thirty to forty smaller gated developments in Accra; many are in the construction phase.

Most of Accra's gated communities are located in the eastern suburbs between the airport and Tema (the main port in Ghana) (Map 3.1). There is little evidence of the central city condominium type and elite developments

4. Interview with Alexander Gillett, design director, Trasacco Estates Development Company, February 12, 2004.

TABLE 3.1

INVENTORY OF GATED COMMUNITIES IN GREATER ACCRA, 2004

| Name | Location | Number of homes | Price range (US$) |
|------|----------|-----------------|-------------------|
| ACP Estates | Pokuase | 600 | $58,000–128,000 |
| Alema Court* | Airport RE | 24 | $175,000–210,000 |
| Bougainville Estate | Baatsonaa | 49 | $30,000–39,000 |
| Cantonment Gardens | Cantoments | 20 | $350,000 |
| Casa Bella | Agbleshia | 25 | $42,000–55,000 |
| Cedar Court* | Airport RE | 18 | $350,000 |
| Devtraco Villas | Baatsonaa | 200 | $30,000–65,000 |
| East Airport | Airport RE | 600 | $96,000–273,000 |
| Ivy Court* | Spintex | 15 | $63,000–90,000 |
| Kwabenya | North Legon | 350 | $26,000–62,000 |
| Lagoon View Estates | Sakumono | 44 | $44,000–180,000 |
| Manet Cotttage Annex | Baatsonaa | 83 | $58,000–110,000 |
| Manet Court | East Airport | 250 | $63,000–110,000 |
| Mariville Homes | Spintex | 240 | $55,000–90,000 |
| Masonia Green | Okpoi Gonno | 60 | $45,000–228,000 |
| Palm Court* | Airport RE | 15 | $250,000 |
| Royal Palms | East Airport | 88 | $141,000–191,000 |
| Spintex Road (Tracof) | Spintex | 40 | $40,000–45,000 |
| Tema Community 18 | Tema | 300 | $40,000–60,000 |
| Tema Community 19 | Tema | 248 | $48,000–60,000 |
| Tracof | Bawalishie | 120 | $23,400–26,000 |
| Trasacco Valley | East Legon Ext. | 300 | $240,000–460,000 |
| Vista Valley | Spintex | 54 | $85,000–135,000 |

Sources: Daily Graphic 1983–2004); various real estate brochures (ACP Estate 2004; Manet 2004; Regalon 2004, Regimanuel Gray 2004; Royal Palms 2004; Taysec 2004; Trasacco Valley 2004).

*Apartments, 2 and 3 bedroom.

that are prominent in gated enclaves in Latin American cities. The heavy concentration of gated communities in the vicinity of the airport is a unique feature of the residential geography of Accra. Although the earliest gated communities catered to the upper end of the housing market, the newest planned communities have targeted the middle class; houses are priced at around US$26,000, close to the average of private developer-built houses. Nevertheless, this is a considerable sum for residents of a country in which average annual per capita income is around US$400.

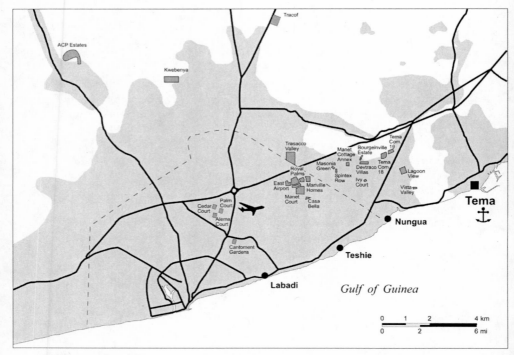

Map 3.1. Geography of Gated Communities in Accra. Sources: Maloney 2004, 30; Daily Graphic 1983–2004; various real estate brochures (ACP Estates 2004, Manet 2004, Regalon 2004; Regimanuel Gray 2004, Royal Palms 2004, Taysec 2004, Trasacco Valley 2004).

*East Airport Gated Community*

The East Airport residential community became the first gated development in Accra. There are three gated communities within the entire residential development. The first community, named Golden Gate, was developed between 1993 and 1995. The second was developed in two phases; Silver Bells Gate 1 in 1998–2000 and Silver Bells Gate 2 in 1998–2001. The third community, Platinum Place, is in the latter phase of its development in 2005, with an anticipated completion date of 2006. By this time, 600 houses will be located inside the three gated communities.

East Airport has been developed by Regimanuel Gray, the largest property developer in Ghana. This JV company combines Regimanuel, a

Ghanaian partner with local experience in the construction and hospitality industries, and Gray Construction, a Houston, Texas-based construction company with international expertise and capital.

This residential project is located seven miles from the center of the city. Residences offered are three- and four-bedroom detached bungalows with separate quarters for house staff on plot sizes up to 100 square feet. Fourteen house types and seven quarters models (for domestic help, etc.) are available, all entailing similar architectural designs and features to ensure the project's homogeneity. Conformity is also maintained by limiting the exterior painting of houses, walls, and gates to four approved colors. A premium is placed on planning order, and all internal streets have been named and signposted with consecutive house numbers. Moreover, this has enabled the developer to finalize the first service agreement in the country with *Ghana Post* for home mail delivery for a modest annual fee. Residential owners opting for this service are fitted with a standard postbox for twice-weekly delivery. All of these ordering features are considered normal in planning schemes in the developed world but not in West Africa.

To maintain the environment, a monthly maintenance and security fee of US$85 is charged to all homeowners. Regimanuel Gray has assumed the role of a property management company, taking care of all security services, landscaping, exterior maintenance, and letting arrangements, but there are plans to contract a private security firm to take on the protection role once the development is complete. There are rules about renting, whereby the property management company handles all leases and liaises with the RA in establishing rules for community living (e.g., speed limits for vehicles, visitor and guest procedures, pets, and noise protocols). The RA meets monthly as well as on a need-be basis. The newness of the community means that rules are still being established. Evidence of this abounds, and official signage around the community has available space for new rules.

The residential development includes a number of amenities, such as a clubhouse, a swimming pool, children's playgrounds, and a worship center. The property developer has sold a triple lot to the Methodists, indicating the commercialization of all aspects of the real estate market. The developer also has future plans for a shopping center, luxury hotel, golf course, and private school for inside the enclave. When all of the services are completed,

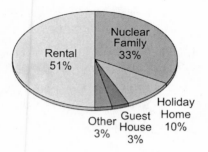

Figure 3.4. Main Purpose of Houses in East
Airport. Source: Grant 2004.

East Airport will function as a self-contained, edge-city-like community (Garreau 1991).

A significant feature of East Airport is the high number of homeowners who live abroad and are nonresidents. Interviews with the property developer estate officer and the RA revealed that 70 percent are nonresident and 30 percent are resident.[5] Of permanent residents, 85 percent are resident Ghanaians and 15 percent are foreigners.

My survey of heads of households asked about the main purpose of the house (Fig. 3.4). About half of the houses are rental investments. One-third use their house for a nuclear family, and 10 percent as a holiday home (typically a second home), but some used the property as a guest house (whereby business associates use it). More important, none of the respondents used the home as a traditional "family home."

The RA confirmed the high proportion of rental properties in the enclave. While Regimanuel Gray did not intend the community to become a rental one, it caters to this demand and advertises "the community as a prime rental investment opportunity" (Regimanuel Gray 2004, 3). In June 2004, monthly rents ranged from US$1,400 to US$2,500, depending on the house. The shortage of well-serviced rental houses in Accra means rentals obtain premium prices, and when rents are paid in foreign exchange (as opposed to the local cedi currency) it is very lucrative for owners. Many nonresident owners use rental investments as a vehicle to afford them an eventual opportunity to live in the residential developments; this is especially true for overseas Ghanaians that intend to return to Ghana.[6]

5. Interview with estate officer Dickson Segbefia and RA, February 13, 2004.

6. Interview with Violet Odoi, executive secretary, Regimanuel Gray, February 16, 2004.

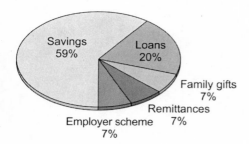

Figure 3.5. How Residents Paid for Their Houses in East Airport. Source: Grant 2004.

Home purchase was largely financed by the owner's own savings (59 percent of houses were paid for out of savings), and about 20 percent of purchase costs was paid for by mortgages and loans. Family gifts and assistance from employer-based schemes were also important to some individuals. Nearly all of the respondents had spent time working abroad, and most confirmed the significance of international investments, remittances, and family earnings abroad to pay for the house.

Residents surveyed about why they decided to live in this area had two distinct responses. Homeowners noted the quality of the project, the investment potential, the high caliber of other residents, prestige, and location. Many renters emphasized that their employer had rented the property for them. Respondents noted that a key factor in deciding to live in the development was that other known high-level professionals and high-profile individuals had already purchased a house there. As one respondent put it, "We bought [a house] here because we knew that well-connected people were already living in this community and being neighbors would enhance our networking in the business community."[7] The property developer confirmed that buyers are very curious about their neighbors prior to making a deposit on a house. The "prestige effect" of the community was mentioned by most of the respondents when they were asked what they liked about the enclave. The majority of residents evaluated the residential area in positive terms, although it was noted that some tensions existed between nonresident and resident owners, particularly over priorities during the completion of the project. Most resident owners wanted all schools and amenities to be finished

7. Interview with gated community resident who wishes to remain anonymous, February 14, 2004.

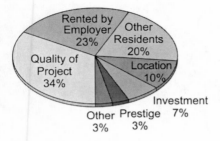

Figure 3.6. Reasons Why Residents Moved into East Airport. Source: Grant 2004.

before any plans were firmed up to attract a hotelier into the area. The high levels of absentee owners and of rental tenants were seen as undermining the community within the community.

Building on the commercial success of the East Airport enclave, Regimanuel is now building additional enclave communities in Tema (e.g., Tema Communities 18 and 19), where prices are considerably lower with more modest monthly association fees (approximately US$5). To keep maintenance costs to a minimum, the RA organizes internal security, whereby individuals contribute their own time to guarding the gate. Regimanuel Gray is also expanding the geographical scope of its enclave projects; others are under consideration in Togo, Benin, Liberia, and Tanzania.

### Trasacco Valley Gated Community

Trasacco Valley, the most expensive gated community in Ghana, is located eight miles from the city center. The land was initially purchased from the Teshie-Nungua clan, and the original aim was to use it for an industrial development. In 1996, the new owner instead decided to build for residential purposes because of the profitability of the upper-income housing market. The residential project has been developed by the Trasacco Group, an amalgamation of five domestic companies that had previously concentrated on building materials and design industries. The 502-acre project is based on "a garden city" master-planned community. It involves a UK architect with international experience in the development of gated communities in Malaysia. The first house was completed in 1999.

Individual housing units are priced at US$240,000–$460,000. Sixteen house models are offered with elaborate names like the King, the Queen, the

President, the Prince, the Princess, and the Tsar. Varying plot sizes are available up to 0.9 acres. Houses are customized to owners' needs and requests, all come with standard staff quarters, and upgrades are available on request (e.g., video entry phone, within-home guardhouses, and electric gates).

The area will include resort amenities, a post office, shops, restaurants, and educational facilities when completed. Agreements are being finalized with the local municipal authority, Tema Metropolitan Assembly, for an on-site police station. Security is currently provided by a privately contracted security company, and an intercom system operates between the gatehouses and each residence. Following the lead of the East Airport enclave, the developer has also finalized a similar agreement for home postal deliveries with *Ghana Post*. The developer has not yet applied the monthly maintenance fee, but a fee will be implemented within two years, when the project is completed. In the meantime, the developer has established an estate management company to oversee services, liaise with residents, and maintain standard community rules. The developer has suggested that "it might be prepared to refund monies to those who do not suit the community."[8] Once the project is complete, the developer will hand over responsibilities to the RA.

The project has primarily targeted Ghanaian high-income earners abroad, particularly celebrities (e.g., soccer players) who want to own a property in a well-serviced residential area. This luxurious enclave development has been regularly advertised in publications with international circulations, such as *African Millionaire* and *Ovation International* (Africa's celebrity magazine). Not surprising, the residential scheme has a 15 percent occupancy rate because most owners use their home as a second residence. Ghanaians own 65 percent of the houses and foreigners own 35 percent. The survey also revealed that 74 percent of houses were paid for with savings and most of the remainder by mortgages. Half of these mortgages were obtained abroad (outside the HFC program), illustrating the owners' earnings outside of Ghana. Moreover, 80 percent of those surveyed owned additional properties abroad, and half of the households owned additional residential properties in Accra.

8. Interview with Ian Morris, project manager, February 14, 2004.

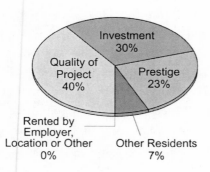

Figure 3.7. How Residents Paid for Their Houses in Trasacco Valley. Source: Grant 2004.

The primary motivations of residents for moving into the development were, in rank order, the quality of the project, investment potential, economic value of the property, prestige, and caliber of other residents. One resident noted that "the prestige and exclusivity of the area is widely known, and for those who can afford it, living in the most exclusive and luxurious residential area in Ghana is a recognition of business success." It is expected that owning a property within the development will become even more prestigious after the hotel and private golf course are completed. (Both will be open to external members and visitors who can afford these services.)

None of the owners used the house as a "family home" or for rental income (Fig. 3.9). The majority viewed the main purpose of the home to be for nuclear families, and the next most frequent perception was for the home to serve as a holiday home. One homeowner noted, "It is crucial to have a secluded residence for close family members to avoid the hassles and headaches of contemporary African city life."

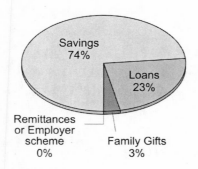

Figure 3.8. Reasons Why Residents Moved into Trasacco Valley. Source: Grant 2004.

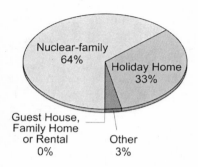

Nuclear-family
64%

Holiday Home
33%

Guest House,
Family Home
or Rental
0%

Other
3%

Figure 3.9. Main Purpose of Houses in Trasacco Valley. Source: Grant 2004.

Although residents view the residential development in positive terms, some negatives were mentioned. Accessibility was viewed as problematic, as was the delay in the project's completion because of various land litigations among the HFC, the local stool, and the developer over some of the boundaries. Some tensions existed among full-time occupants and part-time residents over planning priorities; for example, whether to proceed with building a club house or to move faster in building the luxury hotel and golf course.

## TRANSNATIONAL HOUSES

Clearly dramatic changes are taking place in the residential geography of Accra. The land system is neither a traditional system nor a private market system but somewhere in between. Undoubtedly, a large part of the explanation of how individuals can pay between US$25,000 and US$300,000 for a house when the per capita income is very low and mortgages are scarce lies in the confluence of transnational forces. The local real estate industry is being globalized in parcels, and the large private developers are selling 70 percent of their houses to individuals abroad (mostly Ghanaians) (GIPC 2004a). Others participating in the upper end of the real estate market are circulating sojourners, returning migrants, some locals who have benefitted from the market economy, and local entrepreneurs seeking rental investments. In addition, liberalization policy changes have established the mechanisms allowing individuals to purchase properties from abroad. Most new house purchasers have lived and made money abroad, reinforcing the connection between transnational living and local urban development. A select few (with considerable net worth) have been able to obtain mortgages from lenders abroad. Consequently, the larger private developers have employed international advertising and marketing techniques that have enabled them to pitch upper-income enclave communities to targeted buyers abroad. Furthermore, their professionalism, compared to most of the local informal real estate sector, has made their products even more attractive to those who can afford them.

Urban researchers (e.g., Pellow 2003; Yeboah 2003a) emphasize that globalization offers people the ability to live in two worlds and to create linkages that span borders. Increasing numbers of migrants continue to participate in the economic and social lives of their countries of origin even as they put down roots in destination countries (Levitt 2001). Pellow's (2003) ethnographic research on transmigrating individuals shows that building a home or investing in property reinforces claims on community membership and leads to a rise in social status. Finding evidence of Ghanaians working in places like the Bronx, New York, and building houses in suburban Accra, Pellow (2003, 70) uses the term "transnational house" to describe the phenomenon of transmigrants' split existence of working abroad to build a house in Accra. It is often suggested that, for Ghanaians living abroad, the "dream house" is not in North America but in Accra (Berger 2002). It is inside Accra's gated communities where we find a high prevalence of transnational houses.

Transnational houses are indicative of new economic values for land, for homes, and for community, as well as for the cementing of ties that stretch beyond Ghana's borders. Investment decisions and lifestyle values rather than strict use-value are important motivating factors. Owners have indicated a preference for houses in a community with other professionals. Ethnicity and family ties seem much less important than in an earlier era (Korboe 1992). Segregation by ethnicity appears nonexistent in Ghana, in sharp contrast to the prevailing situation in South Africa (Landman 2004). Houses in gated communities are characterized by more nuclear families and owners more motivated by global lifestyle than by traditional culture considerations. However, this does not preclude owners from also having a family home as well in Accra. It appears that many of the owners at the very upper end of the housing market want to maintain a foothold in several culture realms: traditional Ghana, globalizing Accra, and the global economy.

CONCLUSIONS

The gated community phenomenon in Accra is a clear example of globalizing processes becoming grounded in the urban economy. These private western-style dwelling spaces are created by "a cut and paste logic: cut from the historical urban experiences of global cities and pasted onto a traditional society and culture, but artfully fashioned to create new globalizing spaces that are distinctive in the urban fabric" (King and Kusno 2000, 44). Perhaps, the most surprising aspect of the advertising and marketing of gated communities is the extent to which they tap into global imaginations and how little they draw on traditional conceptions of home, house, and community.

The form and internal structures of Accra's gated communities are similar to global trends: the preference for villa-style houses accompanied by various services and leisure activities. These urban enclaves stand apart in the Accra urban environment as "artful fragments for the culture of stylish materialism" (Knox 1993, 226). Their spatial ordering is particularly amplified in a residential environment, where informal building without any requisite services has been the norm. However, there are two important local differences from the global trends. First, in Accra more emphasis is placed on defensible spaces in a planning sense (e.g., registered titles, fully serviced, planning order) and less on physical security (e.g., walls, barriers, policing). These differences reflect the initial stage in the transformation of the urban land market as well as the particular low-crime environment. Second, most house purchasers have lived and worked abroad. Many currently earn their livings outside of Ghana but also own property in an Accra gated community.

All gated communities, to date, have been built on land that has been purchased from traditional landowners. They represent the ongoing transformation in the urban land market and a globalizing real estate market space within a traditional land-ownership system. Gated communities appear to be a dynamic real estate product with a guaranteed exchange value (US dollars) compared to the lack of a real estate market that prevails in much of residential Accra (but the latter also appears to be changing). The extent to which outsiders are active participants in the local real estate market raises concerns about national economic policies, local planning capabilities, the future of home ownership, the survival of the traditional land system, local community impact, and the sustainable development of the city. Also, the spatial withdrawal of elite groups undermines the contractual neighborhood; between neighbors understanding neighborhood shared values and neighborhood attributes and existing relationships with municipalities (Atkinson and Blandy 2006). Instead, new relationships are developed between the private enclave, the city, and the market. Gated communities are bound to become very controversial in Accra.

There have always been inequalities in housing in Ghana but not to the extent that currently prevails. Presently there is a huge scarcity of affordable houses in the midst of a real estate boom. As Tuurosong (2004, 1) put it, "Foxes have holes and birds of the air have nests but sons and daughters of Ghana have no place to lay their heads. You find them in uncompleted buildings, or sleeping under trees." Accra's new gated communities (built with imported materials and imported funds) are of a different order and magnitude.

The gap between the realms of the traditional houses and of the transnational houses is widening. Gated developments differ from previous exclusive housing areas in five important aspects. First, homeowners opt to live in a private as opposed to a traditional community. Second, homeowners draw on material resources from across the globe to pay for their houses rather than rely solely on national or local resources. Third, the residential schemes are very different in terms of the quality of services provided, infrastructure, and planned layouts; designs are based on housing models developed in North America and elsewhere. Fourth, they typify an entrepreneurial and corporate from of urban governance where municipal authorities rely on private companies to manage neighborhood management functions and utilize public-private partnerships on policing and mail delivery. Fifth, transnational homeowners live in gated communities so they control as much as possible the terms of their engagement with the city and its citizens. For instance, gated communities employ corporate structures in attempting to govern themselves. Transnationals insulate themselves within gated communities to keep, in their minds, the uncontrollable "African city" at bay.

Of course, the contribution of transnationals to local development is still very much mediated by the government policies, and current government policies seek to strengthen the interconnections. A Ghana Homecoming Summit was held in 2001 to harness global Ghanaian resources for national and local development. The Ghana Dual Citizenship Act (2002) was implemented to further strengthen ties. Investment legislation is designed with en eye to foreign participation in the local real estate market. For example, GIPC ACT 1994, Act 478, article B allows a real estate tax exemption for foreign companies on profits from the sale of residential houses or rents for the first five years of operation (GIPC 2004b). Transnational houses are now a salient part of the globalizing city. Their presence adds to the diversity of the city, albeit from behind the walls and the gates. As a medium and outcome, they reveal new housing aspirations among the residential elite. In Anthony King's (2004) words, these are "the globurbs" within the contemporary globalizing African city.

Many questions remain for investigation. Do gated communities represent cognitive and mental walls for urban residents? What do gated communities mean for community, individualism, strangers, and urban society? Which is the precise relationship between local municipal authorities and individual communities (e.g., Who owns the roads? Who is responsible for public services in these communities? Who will pay for upgrades once they are needed?) Will transnationals ever take up full-time residence in the gated communities, or are they dependent on split existence? How will local housing tastes and lifestyles be influenced by the spread of gated communities? There is significant evidence that gated developments are being extended toward the middle-class market. Indeed a number of private developers have residential projects under construction that will target the middle class. Nevertheless, the sharp contrast between the appearance of 3 percent of dwellings in elite gated communities and 60 percent of dwellings in slums is particularly troubling. For many urbanites spaces of hope are now imagined in terms of diaspora living; opportunities that lie beyond Ghana's borders appear to be the only way that they too will be able to afford "dream houses" in enclave communities.[9]

9. Thanks to Dr. Ian Yeboah, Miami Ohio, for suggesting this point.

# 4

# Globalizing from Above and in Between

## *The Residential Building Boom*

> They come in with bags of money and/or they can transfer funds within weeks. The sums are so huge that they have to originate in the United States or Europe.[1]

> I know of a courier that brings in money from Nigeria every other week, and I can point out new houses and new additions that have been paid for with this money.[2]

> Remittances are larger than foreign aid or foreign investment flows. Remittances in recent years are second after exports in terms of resource flows. We believe that we have captured the largest flows but we are also aware that we miss many of the smaller sums that are professionally couriered, brought in by relatives or circulated within families and within companies.[3]

IN SO MANY WAYS, Accra's residential building boom is a huge information lacuna. The scale and extent of residential building along with the topic of housing affordability have become hot button issues in Ghanaian national politics. Already, presidential candidates and parties are espousing strong

1. Interview with real estate agent who wished to remain anonymous, February 16, 2004.
2. Interview with builder who wished to remain anonymous, October 3, 2005.
3. Interview with representative from Bank of Ghana, July 11, 2003.

positions on housing issues in the run up to the December 2008 national elections (Ghanaweb 2006b). With housing costs sky high compared to local wage levels, investigation is warranted about how individuals can afford to pay US$25,000–US$400,000 for new bungalows in private estates and US$8,800-upward for new compounds (Simone 2004, 203).

Urban housing research on Ghana commonly reveals that home owner-ship is beyond all except the wealthy (Konadu-Agyemang 2001a; Konadu-Agyemang 2001b). Housing indicators also show that Accra is among the most inequitable housing environments in Africa. For example, Accra ranks in the bottom four of African cities with a house price to income ratio of 14:1 and a rent to income ratio of 21:1 in 2001 (UN-Habitat 2003, 274). Even with these circumstances, the Accra new-housing environment wit-nessed explosive growth, registering a 108 percent increase in housing stock between 1984 and 2000 (GSS 2002, 19). This trend has been partially explained by accounting for the houses sold to Ghanaians abroad (Maloney 2004), international transfers of monies into the housing sector (Yeboah 2001) and "long-distance house building" by diaspora wage earners (Diko and Tipple 1992; Pellow 2003), who may number 3 million and include 30 percent of all highly educated Ghanaians (Anarfi et al. 2003). Home purchasing preferences of building the "dream house" in Accra away from their hometowns (Kabki et al. 2004) may also play a significant role. Yeboah (2003a, 117) surmises, "that Ghanaians living abroad now own *half* of the new housing stock in Accra."

The building boom paradox can only be understood by emphasizing that African urbanites increasingly draw on material resources that can span the globe (Simone 2004; Gugler 2004). National data confirm this trend; studies show that aggregate income is only 64 percent of what households are spending (GSS 2003, 57–60). Conventionally, remittances into Ghana were used to pay for funerals, school fees, and for helping out during hard times. More recently, remittances have been deployed for productive invest-ments, for example, starting a business and/or paying for new housing.

In this chapter, I aim to capture and document the creative ways that monies have been transferred into physical investments like buying a house. I utilize a variety of data as well as a household survey and interviews with key informants to shed light on the financing of new housing. I explain how the housing construction sector has been able to produce such a large number of dwellings outside of state support and in a context where there are significant constraints on land supply, mortgages, and information. Much of my questioning of local informants concentrated on persuading them to discuss the links between their local housing investments and income generating activities between and beyond the border. As such, my research efforts respond to calls to better situate households within the global economy (Beaverstock, Hubbard and Short 2004) by providing evidence about the housing money trail.

## THE HOUSING ENVIRONMENT PRIOR TO LIBERALIZATION

Housing in Accra between 1957 and 1983 was primarily determined by local factors and conditions. A small private housing sector existed; government figures reveal that 16 percent of Accra houses were owned by private individuals in 1990 (Table 4.1). Most of this private housing was in close proximity to the upscale European residential areas that were developed during the colonial period. Ghanaian elites, foreign diplomats, and international business owners (small in numbers) lived in private housing.

In the decades after independence (1950–80), the government acquired approximately 15 percent of the land (within the city boundary) for development purposes, and a good portion of this land was used for state housing (Odame-Larbi 1996). The government, as part of its new role in national development, became the main instigator of public sector housing in the city through the construction of bungalows for senior public and civil servants (for police, army, nurses, prison wardens, and customs officials) as public and quasi-government institutions also built housing estates. Between 1957 and 1990, the state sector built 24,000 single household dwellings for employees (Tipple and Korboe 1998, 246). State housing accounted for a 15 percent share of Accra dwelling units (Table 4.1).

The traditional and informal sector supplied the vast majority of housing. Government figures show that 62 percent of all dwellings in Accra were compounds. Traditional urban housing generally comprised compound dwellings, consisting of many small rooms off a private internal courtyard. The compound house typically had an "open sky courtyard leading to rooms,

TABLE 4.1

COMPARISON OF PERCENTAGES OF HOUSING STOCK AND
OWNERSHIP CATEGORIES, 1990 AND 2000

| Housing stock (%) | 1990 | 2000 |
| --- | --- | --- |
| Compound | 62.0 | 42.5 |
| Bungalows | 32.0 | 33.9 |
| Flats/apartments | 1.2 | 8.8 |
| Informal/other | 4.8 | 14.8 |

| Ownership categories (%) | 1990 | 2000 |
| --- | --- | --- |
| Government housing | 15 | 3.96 |
| Private employer | 3 | n/a |
| Renters | 66 | 48.0 |
| Household member | 16 | 37.6 |
| Other | n/a | 10.4 |

Source: Ministry of Local Government 1990; UNDP 1992, 88; GSS 2004.

either directly or through a porch or veranda" (Andersen et al. 2006, 5). The courtyard was the women's domain, serving the purposes of cooking, washing, and could be used for home-based economic activities. Typically, compounds were constructed by informal sector builders on plots that could be referred to as the property of the owners but heads of households only had traditional land rights, which meant dwellings were rarely sold to persons outside of the family. Compound dwellings varied in size; some were single story dwellings and others were multistoried structures. This type of housing was popular because it was "affordable, suited traditional inheritance patterns, and allowed the sharing of services with a finite and known group" (Andersen et al. 2006, 6).

Overall, the residential property market in Accra was small and limited as was the case in most African cities during this time period (Rakodi 1997). A critical dimension to the housing scene in urban Ghana is that land and housing were generally *not* for sale. Few houses were ever bought or sold, although some land speculation took place in the 1970s (Quarcoopome 1992). As shown in the previous chapter, real estate advertisements were rare. This situation was culturally based; land and other real property were the birthright of succeeding generations, rather than being at the disposal of the living (Tipple and Korboe 1998). For the most part, land itself remained community property. Housing research shows that the motivations behind building in urban Ghana were mainly concerned with family obligations, status within the society, and making sure that when individuals grew old, they had a place to stay (Tipple and Willis 1992; Korboe 1992). Possession of a house or houses (especially large houses) conferred "big man" status and possible immortality because the house could be passed onto family descendants and the head of households could fulfill duties toward kinfolk. Lineage obligations meant heads of households preferred large houses that could accommodate up to twenty people, and many lived rent-free (Korboe 1992, 1159).

Despite governmental acquisitions of land for state housing, government was a minor player, and families and stools held parcels of land, even if it was highly contestable. Land was not highly valued in monetary terms. Low-density housing in small, built areas beyond the central city characterized the residential geography of Accra. Population pressures as the city urbanized, combined with shortages of building materials, exacerbated the housing supply problem over time. For instance, Accra's housing stock grew only by 1 percent between 1984 and 1990 (Accra Planning and Development Programme et al. 1992). With new housing construction stifled, the rental sector flourished; by 1990, 66 percent of the city's population rented (Table 4.1) and sleeping under a roof entailed more economic costs. This situation prevailed until 1990 when liberalization policies began to reshape the housing environment in dramatic ways.

The 2000 Population and Housing census provides some clues to main changes in the housing fabric during the liberalization era. Census results reveal that 68,340 new houses were built in Accra since 1984 (GSS 2002). In particular, the housing stock classified as detached and semi-detached houses as well as flats/apartments increased the most. Detached and semi-detached dwellings have increased because they bestow the highest status. The younger generation has come to view compounds as old-fashioned and traditional. Real estate agents point out that housing preferences and tastes have changed forever in Accra. Moreover, real estate professionals project that the gap between the economic value of a villa versus a compound will only compound in time as the housing market incorporates the sea change that have taken place in the cultural attitudes to housing.[4] Another reason for the shift away from compound housing is their limited economic value: they cannot be sold out of the family, ownership-in-common. However, there are individual compound properties that have risen in marketable value in particular Accra locations, e.g., Osu. Transacting marketable compound properties is possible but uncommon because of the multiplicity of co-owners who make it very difficult as well as time consuming, often taking years to finalize a sale. Privacy concerns (no one can receive a visitor without all the residents knowing, and without noise traveling easily among the rooms), as well as a shift away from communal life (sharing food, household chores) toward private living are also factors that have facilitated the demise of compound housing (Andersen et al. 2006).

Map 4.1 shows the spatial patterning of housing and illustrates that compounds are much more heavily concentrated in the inner and older parts of the city, while most of the newer houses areas consist of modern, villa-type bungalows. Moreover, the areas dominated by compound housing are increasing in density as compounds have undergone considerable extension activity while villa-style development ringing the city tends to be much lower density housing.

This evidence confirms Konadu-Agyemang's (2001b) contention that Accra is moving from traditional toward private housing. More important, private ownership[5] registered the largest increase in terms of categories of ownership, rising from 15.5 percent to 37.6 percent. The rental market continues to provide housing for most of the city's population. Again, it is worth emphasizing that these changes proceeded in a macro-liberal economic environment but without a major change in traditional land policy; nonetheless, they appear to be ringing in a property market and putting economic values ahead of cultural values to land.

---

4. Private ownership is the category of ownership employed by GSS. In the 2000 census, the GSS allowed households to select this type of ownership among other choices. In Ghana, private ownership does not exist in a strict legal sense as land remains under a traditional system. Some households have formalized their properties by registration and proper titling; many others have not. Nonetheless, therein lies an inherent paradox.

5. See note 4.

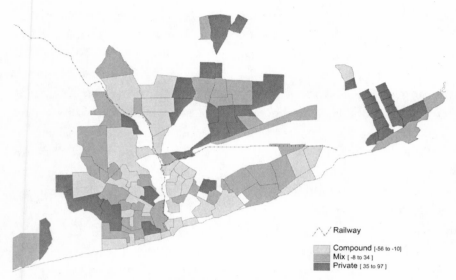

Map 4.1. Residential Geographies of Compound Housing Versus Private Houses in 2000. Source: GSS 2004.

## LIBERALIZATION POLICIES AND CHANGING RESIDENTIAL GEOGRAPHIES

The linkages among economic globalization, urban land markets, and urban residents are both complex and vague. Residential properties involve intricate situations creating diverse networks within national society and beyond. Legislation continues to allow land in Ghana to be transacted within a traditional land policy environment. For example, nationals can acquire land to build houses in ninety-nine-year lease arrangements and foreigners can hold property in Ghana (by fifty-year renewal lease agreements). Strictly speaking, this land is *not* sold, but individuals pay money (market values) to obtain land leases for dwellings, assuming an almost automatic lease renewal once the term expires. Within this framework, land has been both formally (by titles, registration, and permits) and informally (without legal documentation) built upon throughout the city.

An active residential property market has emerged; GIPC estimate that more than 85,000 transactions in residential properties occur per annum (GIPC 2004a, 1). Some researchers (e.g., Hammond 2006, 395) have gone so far as to suggest that "in Accra there is an active purely price operated land and property market comparable to property markets in Western societies." This is probably a stretch but there are considerable investments in bricks and mortar.

Government attempts to stimulate a real estate market began with their withdrawal from housing production, creating a space for large private housing developers to move into. National urban housing policies aimed to increase the number of single household dwelling units rather than multi-habitated compounds (Ministry of Local Government, Government of Ghana 1990). Greater participation of private property developers in the Accra residential market signaled a major break with former traditions and practices. An increased private sector role is reflected in the growing membership GREDA: thirty-eight members in 1988 to 400 in 2003. With World Bank financial support, the government established the HFC in 1991 to initiate a mortgage program.

Aspects of government liberalization policies also delocalized the residential property market. For instance, the HFC and private property developers cooperate in sustaining a mortgage program that is now tailored to wealthier Ghanaians abroad (buyers can borrow up to US$80,000 with a 20 percent down payment). Government policy makers made it a point to urge Ghanaians abroad to invest in the economy. For instance, the HFC has worked out money transfer arrangements between banks in North America and Europe to facilitate mortgage payment transfers among foreign banks, the HFC, and private developer accounts in Ghana. Moreover, as shown in the previous chapter, the liberalization era went hand in hand with vastly improved information on residential projects (e.g., Web sites, brochures, pricing) and efforts to professionalize the local residential markets.

In the liberalization climate, two divergent patterns of new residential development emerged. Formal private housing estates, ranging from 50 units to 600 units were created. This type of housing stands apart in terms of uniformity, planning, and requisite services. Residential estate development costs are high in Accra because 70 percent of project capital is allocated to initial land development, the provision of requisite services, and utilities (Maloney 2004, 16). High per-unit cost of Accra housing results in property developers concentrating on the upper end of the housing market, that is, on individuals in Ghana and those abroad who can afford to pay premium prices for well-serviced residential projects. In particular, property developers target expatriates who are looking for reliable agents in the entire home-building process, and who want to avoid all of the problems in building through informal channels (e.g., having to deputize the building to a relative, friend, or business associate or to manage the building from abroad). We have no way of putting exact figures on the share of private housing but most local housing experts agree it is about 10 percent of Accra housing.

In addition to these estates, there are the areas that have been built by individual builders who erect houses over an expanded time period, taking anywhere from six to fifteen years for completion (Yeboah 2001). Many of these builders have turned to western-style bungalow/villa-type dwellings. These houses are not uniform; they are built to varying construction and architectural standards and usually without appropriate service provisions. A good proportion of this housing is built without proper permits (Antwi and Adams 2003). Shortages of cash/savings and the inability to qualify for the limited national mortgage scheme have made it difficult for many builders to finance new house construction. Construction is generally financed with cash, drawing from a variety of sources such as funds saved from time working abroad, family gifts, brothers and sister's remittances, employer loan schemes, and/or opportunities for favors or cash windfalls (known colloquially as the "Grace of God").

## THE OUTSIDE IN: INWARD INVESTMENTS

The implementation of liberalization policies opened the door for foreign investors. Initially, FDI concentrated on the manufacturing sector, but after 1991 investments began to flow more into the building and residential construction sector. Because of the gateway role of Accra in the Ghanaian economy, 80 percent of FDI was concentrated in the city (GIPC 2004b, 1).

By 2004, 125 companies were active in the building, construction, and real estate development sectors in Accra. This amounts to a US$134 million inward investment, which translates to a 6 percent share of total inward investments (a comparable share of FDI was registered for Shanghai in the early 1990s, prior to the accelerated growth of the housing sector [Wu 2002, 1595]). Early on, most of the FDI concentrated on infrastructure and civil engineering projects, but more recently, many of the large investors have extended the scope of their investments to include the residential property sector. The growth in FDI in residential building has also generated employment. FDI companies in the building sector formally employ more than 10,357 workers, making it the second largest FDI employment sector (after manufacturing) (GIPC 2004b, 10).

The geographical origins of the foreign companies in the residential construction and real estate sector reveal that the recent liberalization era has entailed opportunities for investors from across the world (Table 4.2). Many companies from the developing world (particularly from Lebanon) began investing in the late 1990s, although the largest builders tended to be from the United States and the United Kingdom.

Given the complex and opaque nature of the land environment, most FDI is in the form of JVs. Seventy-three percent of companies participate in the residential building and real estate sector as JV arrangements. Twenty-

TABLE 4.2

THE TOP TWELVE MOST ACTIVE COUNTRIES IN BUILDING CONSTRUCTION AND REAL ESTATE DEVELOPMENT

| Ranking 2004 | Country | Companies |
|---|---|---|
| 1 | Lebanon | 13 |
| 2 | Italy | 13 |
| 3 | UK | 12 |
| 4 | China | 10 |
| 5 | Germany | 9 |
| 6 | India | 7 |
| 7 | USA | 7 |
| 8 | Switzerland | 6 |
| 9 | Canada | 4 |
| 10 | Netherlands | 3 |
| 11 | South Korea | 3 |
| 12 | South Africa | 2 |

Sources: Interviews; GIPC 2006.

Notes: There were 27 multilateral companies, which provide capital from more than one country (i.e., capital comes from several countries). The total number of companies active in the real estate sector was 125.

seven companies combine capital and resources from more than three countries. Typically, in these partnerships the foreign partner(s) put capital up
front and the domestic partner contributes local knowledge and contacts,
equipment, and staff prior to a subsequent capital investment. In JV partnerships, the local contribution is not made public, but in some cases the
financial contribution can be considerable. Few foreign companies invest as
wholly owned foreign companies, as we might expect under the Ghanaian
Land Law and the political sensitivity of the land issue.

Initially, residential builders also provided real estate services in Ghana
(selling, marketing, assisting in obtaining finance, etc.), but since 2001, new
FDI flows have gone into the real estate service sector (management and
consultancy firms in particular). These tend to be smaller investments of $.5
million to $.875 million. For instance, Sethi Realty, a UK/Indian foreign
company, is involved in real estate management for rentals, and Black Star
Development Company, a British Virgin Island foreign company, participates
in real estate consultancy services. Investment in real estate services reflects a
deepening of foreign penetration into the real estate sector.

FDI captures a major formal channel of investment in the housing sector, but it offers a far from complete picture. Money also flows into the residential sector through informal channels such as taking cash themselves,
sending money through relatives or through another person, using online
banking, and through networks of informal agents (e.g., drivers are used
for transporting funds within the West African region, and air couriers
transport money from distant locations). Elites and returnees with adequate
resources for frequent travel abroad are particularly well positioned to shift
investments, and can take advantage of currency movements in timing their
investments (Tiemoko 2004).

New official data collected by the Bank of Ghana indicate that formal
components of the money trail come from abroad. Figure 4.1 shows trends
in private requited funds[6] (remittances). Inward transfers have grown steadily
from US$179 million in 1994 to almost US$.07 billion in 2003 and media

---

6. Private unrequited transfers are transfers from individuals that are sent from outside
the country through a bank or financial institution that reports the value of the monetary
exchange to the Bank of Ghana.

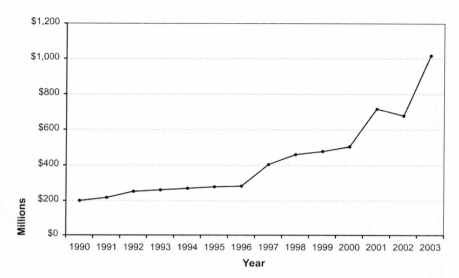

Figure 4.1. Private Unrequited Funds (Remittances) to Ghana. Source: Bank of Ghana 2004.

reports reveal an increase to US$2 billion in 2004. Studies of Ghanaian migrants show an increasing commitment to sending increasing amounts of money (Orozco 2005). In this regard, Ghanaians are similar to Nigerians and dissimilar to migrants from other countries in that the sums of their remittances increase with the length of time spent abroad (Orozco 2005).

The phenomenal growth in remittance flows is explained by the increasing importance of nonaltruistic motivations (in addition to traditional altruistic motivations: family sustenance, school fees, medical care), such as investing and accumulating wealth, house purchase/or assisting family members in new house financing, and diversifying risks between foreign and home country (Addison 2004; Asiedu 2003; Higazi 2005). Since 2001, private requited flows have rapidly expanded and now exceed foreign aid and FDI flows (Addison 2004). The steady growth in remittance to Ghana is similar to a global trend observed in many developing countries. Remittances now register as the third highest foreign exchange earner after gold and cocoa, and private unrequited funds[7] have been increasingly the fastest

7. Interview with representative from Bank of Ghana, July 11, 2003.

growing sector and one of the main sectors of income in the economy. These funds are dispersed throughout the country but the largest share is centered on Accra.

The formal channeling of overseas funds has been facilitated by Ghanaian banks and financial houses, which have become directly involved in remitting monies with foreign affiliate operations from fourteen countries (Table 4.3). Remitting banks/financial houses are mostly concentrated in North America and Western Europe, reflecting both Ghanaian emigration patterns into higher-income countries and the penetration of foreign financial operations into Ghana. Some of these companies have extensive affiliate partners locally. For example, Western Union operated 130 offices in Accra in 2007, and its popularity is a function of it charging lower rates to Ghana (and Nigeria) compared to what it charges in the rest of Africa because of high demand.

Still, it is important to point out that not all flows of investments into the real estate sector are one-way. A number of realtors informed me about Accra land and property deals that were executed in London, New York, and Atlanta. They reported that land and/or property transactions took place outside the country and they speculated "that the exchanged funds were still held in European and North American banks." One realtor put it, "the property market is now so complex that a major deal might be done in London with only a few key individuals being aware of all the details and in a position to reconstruct how the transaction was done. Such funds might never show up in Ghana."[8] One interviewee emphasized that "if this practice became commonplace then the entire real estate market in Ghana could be undermined."[9] No doubt, there are tensions between realtors in Ghana and realtors abroad who conduct transactions in Ghanaian lands. None of the local realtors were directly involved in these "foreign" transactions. These cases are the exception rather than the rule, but provide evidence that land deals have become increasingly complex and secret, and that the money trail can loop outside of Ghana.

8. Interview with real estate agent who wished to remain anonymous, July 12, 2003.
9. Interview with real estate agent who wished to remain anonymous, July 12, 2003.

TABLE 4.3

FOREIGN AGENTS AND THEIR LOCAL PARTNERS
IN MONEY TRANSFERS

| Remitting country | Foreign agent | Ghanaian institution |
|---|---|---|
| USA and UK | First American Remittance | First African Financial Services Ltd. |
| UK | Merchant Foreign Exchange | Amalgamated |
| France | Western Union Financial Services | Ecobank (Gh) Ltd. |
| UK | Express Group International | Express Funds International |
| Italy | Itagha | International Commercial Bank |
| USA | Vigo Remittance Corp. | Merchant Bank |
| UK, Holland, and Belgium | Transcheq Services Ltd | |
| UK | Lawrence Associates | |
| USA | Ecowas | |
| UK | Choice Money Transfer | |
| Canada | Data Connect System | |
| Holland | Afrister | |
| Germany | SOS Express | |
| UK | Kashkall Africa Ltd. | |
| UK | Trans-Continental Financial Services | Metropolitan Allied Bank |
| UK | Samba International | |
| Canada | Linksel Communication | |
| France | Western Union Financial Services | NIB |
| Belgium, Burundi, Croatia, Ireland, Rwanda, and Uganda | First Remit Ltd. | Prudential Bank Ltd. |
| UK | Ghana Express | |
| UK | MoneyGram International | SG-SSB Bank |
| USA | Ria Financial Services | |
| Holland | Unity Financial Services | |
| UK | Kumasi market | Transcontinental Financial |
| Canada | Linkstel Communication | |
| USA and Canada | Uniteller Financial Services | Unibank (Gh) Ltd |

*Source:* Bank of Ghana 2004.

THE INSIDE OUT: HOME BUYERS, HOME PURCHASE,
EMPLOYMENT HISTORY, AND CURRENT OCCUPATIONS

Given the number of new houses in Accra, particularly at the upper end, I surveyed heads of households to obtain data on who is buying new houses, what is their employment history and what is their current occupation? Responses varied depending on the sensitivity of the information asked. As expected, some respondents did not elaborate on details, noting that the information was "too personal," "sensitive," or "secret." Yet, about two-thirds of respondents provided detailed responses to every question.

Figure 4.2 indicates who is "buying property" in Accra. Nonresident Ghanaians own 22 percent of new houses, returnees 25 percent, and others 9 percent (mostly foreign companies). Combined, almost half of this housing has been purchased by individuals who have spent time abroad. Nonresident Ghanaians were found in greater numbers in private estates; 72 percent of all nonresident Ghanaians bought in these areas. This reflects a strong preference to buy from property developers and to hold a property in a new planned estate, avoiding the hassles of land acquisition and subsequent building and reducing the risk that standards may not be upheld on adjacent properties.

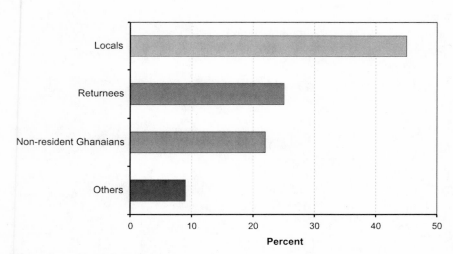

Figure 4.2. Who Is Buying Property in Accra? Source: Grant 2004.

Respondents, who were present during the survey, elaborated on the draw of private estates, such as the quality and clarity of information, the involvement of reliable selling agents, the accompaniment of proper services, architectural models, and planning styles in estate planning that were on par with projects in their host countries. Returnees were found in almost equal numbers in private estates and individual builder areas. Incomes and savings varied widely among returnees, explaining the even split in terms of their selection of where to live. Returnees purchased a house largely based on savings they accumulated abroad. Returnees, in particular, were motivated to purchase a house because they did not see themselves as fitting into the family home, and they felt the pressures of their immediate family to have a separate house. Privacy was a major motivating factor especially for returnees with a foreign spouse and/or children raised abroad.

Outsiders do not own all of the new expensive housing; locals have acquired 40 percent of it, and many of them originate from Accra. Nationals have also moved from nearly all of the regions of Ghana into new Accra housing. Two-thirds of the local purchasers of new houses were in individual built areas. A number of factors are involved. First, housing is more affordable in these areas. Second, incremental construction using informal builders is the norm, helping to keep overall costs to a minimum. Third, locals with family, clan, and community networks are able to acquire plots of land from traditional landowners at a fraction of the cost of land in private communities.

Nine percent of owners are foreign companies. Lacking local networks, they almost exclusively buy in private estates. Most of these houses are owned by companies or company directors, and are used as accommodations for company executives. Foreign companies opt for this housing because the services are comparable to international standards, and the communities are largely composed of similar individuals who have experience abroad. Most of the foreign respondents also emphasized that they "wanted a housing investment that was very liquid" and that could be transacted or rented depending on future circumstances.

Not all buyers purchased new houses for immediate occupancy. Twenty-eight percent of heads of household respondents were renters who paid monthly; another 7 percent were caretakers who were allowed to stay in the house for minimal charges. The rental market in upscale housing has developed in tandem with the sale of expensive houses. Foreign companies' demand for rental houses for their employees and younger private sector employees who rent while saving for home purchase explain a large part high-end rentals. Private developers supply this demand and advertise their communities in promotional materials as prime rental investment opportunities. In May 2004, monthly rents ranged from US$400 in individual unit areas to US$1,200 in private estates and up to US$2,500 in exclusive gated developments. The shortage of well-serviced rental houses in Accra makes it possible for rents to be at premium prices in private estates, and when rents are paid in foreign exchange (as opposed to the local cedi currency) it can be a profitable investment.

In terms of occupational history, nearly all home purchasers had spent some time working outside of Ghana, which supports previous findings (Diko and Tipple 1992; Maloney 2004) of work abroad as the major route to new home ownership. In terms of current occupation, there is a clear shift away from the government sector to the private sector as the main part of the economy providing employment to finance new constructions (Table 4.4). Most homeowners are employed by financial or producer service companies (banking, real estate, management consultancy, etc.).

TABLE 4.4
SECTORAL EMPLOYMENT AND CURRENT OCCUPATIONS
OF HEADS OF HOUSEHOLDS

| Occupation | Private estates (%) | Individual builder areas (%) | Average (%) |
|---|---|---|---|
| Financial and producer services | 60.0 | 23.0 | 41.5 |
| Sales and trade | 20.0 | 30.0 | 25.0 |
| Retired | 10.0 | 12.0 | 11.0 |
| Government | 5.0 | 20.0 | 12.5 |
| Manufacturing | 2.0 | 10.0 | 6.0 |
| Other | 3.0 | 5.0 | 4.0 |
| OF WHICH IS: | | | |
| Domestic | 25.0 | 35.0 | 30.0 |
| Foreign | 65.0 | 55.0 | 60.0 |
| Both | 10.0 | 10.0 | 10.0 |

Source: Grant 2004.

The foreign sector employed 60 percent of heads of households in private estates and another 10 percent were engaged in both the foreign and the domestic sectors. New house purchases are possible because the foreign sector pays the highest wages in Ghana, and many senior managers report that they, in effect, receive two salaries: one in dollars or euros and another in cedis. With nonlocal salaries, they do not suffer from the inflationary effects of the local currency, and, if anything, the strength of foreign currency increases buying power in the Accra housing market, especially when salaries are based on international cost of living indicators. For expatriates as well as Ghanaian workers, salaries that are on par with their counterparts in London, Lagos, and New York can buy a lot more house in Accra, where housing prices are lower by international, but not local, standards.

## FINANCING NEW CONSTRUCTIONS: WHERE IS THE MONEY TRAIL?

Earlier research on the financing of housing showed that formal financing from domestic lending institutions was rare and that most buyers paid for housing from savings and/or borrowed money from family and friends (Tipple et al. 1999). Research on Netherlands-based Ghanaians also shows that most non-Ghanaians invest in housing back home (Kabki et al. 2004) and over three-quarters of Ghanaians in the United States have real estate investments in Ghana (Orozco 2005, 26). To determine where the money came from for new housing investments, I asked respondents how they paid for their purchase, what the sources of their funds were, and what kinds of investments abroad and/or received remittances were used to pay for the initial purchase. Again, these are sensitive questions in any housing environment, and particularly so in Ghana because of cultural norms. Twenty-five percent of respondents in private estates did not provide answers to these questions, and one-third of respondents in individual builder areas were nonresponsive to the same questions. Nonrespondents also included two heads of households who credited the "Grace of God" and two who identified a "Foreign Aunty" as a source of funds but would not elaborate.

Individuals paid for housing mainly from their savings (Figure 4.3). Certainly migrants who earned income abroad and accumulated savings were in a good position to take advantage of improvements in the investment climate in Ghana. Savings were mainly accumulated in North American and Western European countries. Higher accumulations of savings were reported for individuals who worked in the United States. This may account for estimates that half of Ghana's migrants now head to the United States (Black, King and Litchfield 2003, 6). Respondents also accumulated savings from working in Lebanon, Nigeria, Togo, and Benin, and a few reported accumulated savings from time spent in South Korea, Malaysia, and China. Less than 20 percent of the funds came from loans from banks/financial institutions. Remittances provided about 10 percent of funds for the initial investment. Family gifts accounted for 9 percent and are still an important source of income.

There is an emerging divergence between older houses in Accra that have been acquired through traditional local mechanisms (inheritance and family savings based on local economic activities) and new structures that have been built with savings and funds invested from abroad. This is not to suggest that houses are financed exclusively by either local or global sources, but there are considerable financial costs involved in plot acquisition, building materials, and labor, and these costs have increased disproportionately to local wages. Employer schemes were important to some home buyers, but these schemes varied widely. In private estates, foreign companies assisted senior personnel in house purchases, but more commonly foreign corporations purchased one or two houses and used them for their high-level employees, who lived rent-free as part of a relocation package. In individual builder areas, domestic companies (especially banks) have continued the tradition of employer schemes for assisting employees in new home purchases. These efforts typically entail the building of a cluster of several houses in specific residential areas.

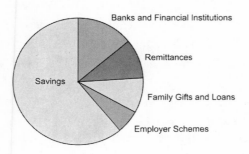

Figure 4.3. How Individuals Pay for New Houses. Source: Grant 2004.

In housing research on Ghana, a common assumption is that new house construction is the ultimate investment where all sources of funds are pooled to realize the purchase. My surveys confirm that this is the case for about 40 percent of the surveyed population. Housing investments for this group generally center on retirement as the ultimate goal and/or on keeping future financial options open. More important, the majority framed their housing investment within a broader investment relationship. A select group of wealthy individuals regarded the house as part of a large investment portfolio, and they were able to focus on investments abroad after making the Accra housing investment.

Most respondents acknowledged the immediate economic benefit that they accrue from housing investing. For instance, they noted the economic benefits of being able to find renters for rooms or to build additional structures on the property, if tolerated by the locality (e.g., extensions, apartments, kiosks). Many respondents noted the economic aspects of owning a house in terms of an inheritance asset that can be passed on to nuclear family members.

Not all of the investments abroad were held by foreigners, nonresident Ghanaians, or returnees. A major surprise in the findings was that one-third of the investments abroad were held by locals, all of whom maintained foreign and domestic bank accounts, and many held stocks and other assets abroad. This is in striking contrast to reports that less than 5 percent of Ghanaians have bank accounts (Orozco 2005).

Locals maintained business interests abroad, and many are able to circulate investments in and out of Accra (presumably maximizing profits and interest rate variations and utilizing tax regimes). There is a considerable range in the type and scale of investments. Examples of the large investments (more than US$100k) are auto importing (United States, United Kingdom, South Korea), and building and construction (Germany, the Netherlands, South Africa and Lebanon). Medium investments (ranging from US$5k to US$99k) include retail investments (United States) and those of licensed independent building and construction contractor firms (Netherlands, Germany, United Kingdom). Examples of smaller investments (less than US$10K) include the import of used clothing (Europe), foodstuffs, courier services (Nigeria and the West Africa region), herbal medicines (China) and savings/brokerage accounts (Europe and North America). About 20 percent of individuals with investments abroad were active in more than one country.

The specifics of some individuals' investments are provided below in five profiles:

• Male, 45, returnee, has owned a house in a private estate since 1999. He paid for house income earned abroad. He repays some family loans out of profits from a secondhand car dealership in Accra and investments in partner car enterprises in London and New York. He receives weekly income of minimum US$125 from entrepreneurial activities abroad as well as substantial income from local entrepreneurial activities.

• Male, 46, nonresident Ghanaian, owns a house in a private estate and a number of Internet cafes and phone call enterprises in New York City. A family member takes care of the house and lives rent-free. The house was paid for out of savings earned abroad. He intends to occupy the house on retirement.

• Male, 59, U.S. citizen, rents in a private estate and works in the airlines service industry. He has an investment in a shopping mall development in Las Vegas. He is in the process of purchasing a new house in Accra and intends to live in the house but plans to sell it after five years and make considerable profits.

• Woman, 57, local, inherited father's house in middle-income area in 2003. She has an import-export trade partnership with Lagos business partners. This arrangement entails maintaining investments in the Nigerian part of the operation. Business connections abroad generate US$125 per week in addition to local profits generated in the informal sector.

• Woman, 41, local, owns a house in middle-income area since 2003. She is an entrepreneur in textile import-export trade. Her business interests in Europe involve a textile wholesaling operation centered in Germany and an informal building and construction company (the hires some Ghanaians) in the Netherlands. She reports that most of her income is made outside of Ghana. Profits have paid the cost of building her house, and the remainder has been lodged in a European financial institution.

Still the standard investment model that concentrates on the individual household and the economics of investment decisions does not fully explain investment patterns. Many respondents detailed secondary social benefits that accrue from a housing investment: an increase in social status in Ghana, family recognition, and self-fulfillment by their active participation in national development. It was also emphasized that the extended family derived indirect benefits (benefits distinct from directly investing in the Ghanaian-family home in their hometown or in a separate Accra location) from their housing investment. The new house often became the urban node in family networks that extended overseas (where packages, mail, messages, and sometimes e-mail could be received and transmitted from). Some realized parts of family financial obligations by allowing family members to operate small businesses from the property and by permitting their address to be used for job applications and other activities. It was reported that investing in a new expensive house sent a signal about their resources and commitment to the Ghanaian family. According to one male respondent, "my new house signals to my entire family that I am around and can be counted on in times of emergencies and crises."[10] Signaling in individual builder areas meant that housing investments indirectly benefitted the extended family's position, in particular its access to informal credit. It was also reported that large housing investments enabled extended family members to realize benefits in the marriage market. Several interviewees claimed that their sister married well because their new house "sent a signal that they were an up and coming family in Accra."[11]

CONCLUSIONS: GLOBALIZING FROM ABOVE AND IN BETWEEN

My findings support those who have argued for some time that the global economy is of major importance in explaining trends in housing at the upper end in Accra (e.g., Diko and Tipple 1992; Yeboah 2003). Those who make their livelihood in the foreign sector own most of these new houses: nonresident Ghanaians, foreigners, and locals who are heavily engaged in the

10. Interview with head of household "Arnold" who wished to remain anonymous, May 17 2005.

11. Ibid.

international sector. My research shows that approximately 43 percent of the houses in private estates, and almost 30 percent of those in individual builder areas, are owned by returnees and/or by foreigners/foreign companies. My findings show tandem but separate movements in a globalizing economy; it creates opportunities for outsiders to buy affordable houses by international price comparisons, and it enables some locals to engage in economic activities beyond the borders and to utilize profits from these investments to finance new house constructions. In many ways, in-between globalizing activities in housing are a coping strategy for navigating an unaffordable residential market. The materialization of these efforts goes beyond the actual building of houses; the process is reshaping economic and social relationships. Simultaneously, heads of households embed themselves in broader globalizing processes while participating actively in making new residential geographies.

My investment approach to understanding the new upper-income Accra housing phenomenon provides two important insights. First, it emphasizes an explicit entrepreneurial aspect to housing investments. Elites are increasingly framing their housing investments as part of a broader investment relationship. Second, it confirms claims that individuals are selectively redefining and reconfiguring family relationships and commitments (see, for example, Mohan 2006). There is an obvious deep politics in the sense of obligations to extended families and home communities in a society where land remains largely under traditional land arrangements. Wealthier individuals in the Accra housing market separate the Ghanaian-family home from the nuclear family home but claim that their housing investment signals their commitment to extended family members, albeit in an indirect way.

The preference for villa low-density housing and now seemingly nuclear family dwellings prompts many policy questions. Can the private sector deliver housing for the poor? What can replace the gaping hole in the delivery system with the demise of compound housing (Andersen et al. 2006)? Is there any future for compound dwellings? Is affordable housing possible in the new globalizing environment? Will housing authorities, developers, and architects be able to create a new form of housing with the advantages of compound housing that also fits into the new realities of a globalizing city?

We have no way of knowing how sustainable or transient transnationalism in housing will be. Moreover, we can only speculate on how transformative it may be. It seems reasonable to conclude that the housing market of Ghanaians abroad, which has reflected Accra as a residential location (over alternative national locations), may have peaked in 2005. It is unknown if wealthier Ghanaians who have worked and lived abroad will continue to want to retire to Ghana. We also do not know if locals will continue to succeed with their investments abroad and whether they will continue to channels investments into the housing sector. The Accra upper-income housing market may have topped along with most of the global housing market. It remains to be seen if additional wealthy emigrants could be tapped to continue the housing boom (Zachary [2005, 9] found 1,000 African Americans residing in the city). However, much may depend on the general economic climate of the West African region and on the role of Accra as a regional gateway.

In an earlier time and writing specifically about Asante property in Kumasi, Sara Berry (2000) emphasized the "family secrets" in determining who had access to and ownership of land. She acknowledged the lack of hard data (maps and documents) to verify land ownership but highlighted the role of local expert knowledge, typically of the chiefs. The liberalization era privileges a different expertise and entails its own secrets: namely, how heads of households have been able to find plots, to build, and to pay for new houses. The current housing environment is an imperfect market in terms of available information, expertise, and transparency. Navigating this imperfect market requires specialized knowledge, networks (both domestic and foreign), and foreign cash. New motivations, particularly consumption and investment opportunities, appear to be important. In many instances, housing investment is part of a larger investment relationship that crisscross international borders. The fact that there is evidence of Accra land deals that have been executed abroad is a good illustration of the new environment. Many of the transnational activities are delocalizing important segments of the local residential property market, adding another dimension to existing uneven residential geographies and changing the city forever. The various impacts (economic, social, political, etc.) of transnational investments on the housing scene remain an important area for further inquiry.

# 5

# In-Between Globalizing

*Returnees' Networks and Spaces*

SOME RETURN MIGRANTS TO GHANA are recognized for making significant contributions to national development. One of the most celebrated returnees is Patrick Awuah, a Microsoft Corporation millionaire, who returned to Accra with his Seattle-born wife after twenty years of residence in the United States to establish a private, western-styled, higher learning institution—Ashesi University.[1] Launching this effort in Accra, Mr. Awuah contributed half a million dollars from his own savings. *The Chronicle of Higher Education* labeled this new and small university as "a Swarthmore transplanted to Africa" (Kigotho 2004). Subsequently, Mr. Awuah was named the "2005 Person of the Year" by Ghanaweb for his efforts to build an African Ivy League university (GhanaWeb 2006b) whose aim is to graduate a new generation of ethical, entrepreneurial leaders.

Ashesi University stands apart from Ghana's national universities in that its advisory board comprises both international advisors from U.S. universities (e.g., University of California, Berkeley, Swarthmore, University of Washington) as well as domestic advisors from Ghanaian private business and academic communities. Contemporary returnees, like Patrick Awuah, emphasize an explicitly economic mobilization of entrepreneurship, capable of transcending all boundaries. Present-day returnees seem very different from the postindependence returnee generation, who exclusively sought

---

1. Ashesi University was inaugurated in 2002, and is a subsidiary of Ashesi University Foundation, a nonprofit, publicly supported U.S. corporation based in Seattle, Washington. Ashesi means "beginning" in the Akan language.

nation-building within the parameters and borders of the Ghanaian state (Ammassari 2004). Some posit that the deep pockets of returnees' investments (in "bootstrap enterprises" and new housing constructions) are ushering in a new development paradigm (Machan 2005, 1).

There is a significant literature on the experience of Ghanaian migrants abroad. The migration process of back and forth traffic usually facilitates learning about new markets and different cultural values (Mazzucato 2005) and can build connections straddling national borders. In some instances, new paths of economic mobility can materialize, whereby migrants take on transnational entrepreneurial roles (Portes et al. 2002). Research on Ghanaians abroad (Arhinful 2001; Tiemoko 2004; Orozco 2005) has shown that migrants often resist some traditions. For example, property rights, family obligations, and social networks are often recast. Inherently, a tension emerges between the dual roles of fulfilling extended family obligations and those of self and/or nuclear family, leading to a politics over commitments (Mohan 2006), and particularly over whom is included and excluded (Henry and Mohan 2003; Mohan 2006).

Much less is known about return migrants. In many ways, returnees are the *missing* and *unknown agents* in understanding the globalizing city. Returnees are extremely hard to track because governments do not record systematic data about them. Existing research shows that most returnees relocate to the most globally connected, urban center (Cohen 2005). Evidence from Ghana shows that not only do returnees relocate to Accra, but their investments are also concentrated there. For instance, research on Ashanti return investments revealed a strong Accra concentration to the detriment of the Ashanti city of Kumasi (Smith and Mazzucato 2003; Kabki et al. 2004; Mazzucato et al. 2006).

In terms of a transnationalism lens, return migrants represent an in-between group. Potentially their networks are neither exclusively rooted in the initiatives of immigrants themselves (i.e., "from below,") nor dependent on institutional actors and external agents (i.e., "from above"). The theoretical literature (Levitt and Glick Schiller 2004; Jackson et al. 2004) posits that traditional social networking and transnational networking are neither incompatible nor binary opposites; rather, they are combined. In theory, returnees are expected to combine transnational networking, preexisting family networks, and new networks with neighbors and other associates.

In this chapter I document the core roles of returnees in terms of housing and business investments. I explore the types of networks that develop around these investments and examine the politics of inclusion and at various geographical scales. I emphasize new houses that have been built by returnees as opposed to traditional Ghanaian- family houses (built to serve family events and to provide accommodation for the wider family). I employ a social field perspective to examine networks (Levitt and Glick Schiller 2004), and I combine it with Hanson's conceptualization of the most important fields of networking in urban Ghana (Hanson 2005).

## EXPLORING RETURNEE NETWORKS: COMBINING CORE INVESTMENT DECISIONS AND A SOCIAL FIELD PERSPECTIVE

As already shown in the previous chapter, significant foreign funds have flowed into the Accra residential housing sector. Migration research also shows that three-quarters of Ghanaians living in the US have a real estate investment in Ghana (Orozco 2005, 26), and many dream about returning home. I identified motivations for housing investments in earlier chapters, combining economic and cultural factors. However, returnees' housing investments may be even more complex. There are added expectations that successful returnees should build a nuclear family house (given that they may be accustomed to living separate) as well as a Ghanaian-family house, and that they should contribute to national economic environment.

Besides investing in houses, returnees start all kinds of "bootstrap economic enterprises." This business environment is every bit as murky as the housing environment. Little information exists, few business directories are available (*FIT Business Directory* is an exception), and business support programs are modest, at best. Returnees poorly prepared for entrepreneurial activities also worsen the situation. Oftentimes, entrepreneurial ventures represent a complete break in career paths and returnees rely on friends and family for information (to identify business opportunities, establish contacts, and support and assess risk) (Portes et al. 2002). According to Portes et al. (2002), typically, the idea for microenterprises originates with the migrant's experiences abroad and the investment capital comes from the migrant's personal savings. Two types of business investment paths are the norm in Ghana. The first is locally based, microenterprises, for example, small restaurants, video stores, auto sales and repairs, personal services, laundromats, and office supplies (Black, King and Tiemoko 2003). The second is import-export businesses, for example, secondhand parts, cars, and clothing (Smith and Mazzucato 2003), often relying on business connections abroad.

I apply a social field perspective to frame the spatiality of Accra returnees' networks. Networks can be defined as "a set of multiple interlocking networks of social relationships through which resources, ideas, and practices are unequally exchanged, organized, and transformed" (Levitt and Glick Schiller 2004, 1009). This operationalization allows me to combine investment decisions and domains of interaction. My approach ascribes a central role to simultaneity in terms of involvement in networks straddling a variety of geographical locations and connecting various geographical scales, e.g., neighborhood, city, and international. Adding a relevant dimension to the globalizing city, I anticipate that national boundaries will not bind Accra returnee networks. Instead, I anticipate that their social fields will stretch across multiple sites simultaneously (tribal-rural, tribal/rural-urban, and international-urban).

It is important to note that the number of transnational ties does not necessarily reflect the depth of the ties. The ties that bind can, however, be assessed by in-depth interviews. Following Hanson's (2005) conceptualization of networking in urban Ghana, I examine 1. family-kin networks based on the "new house," 2. entrepreneurial networks based on a recently established "bootstrap enterprise," and 3. neighborhood networks anchored from the new house. I draw on his notion of fictive kin—"the widespread practice of elevating longstanding friends to the status of family members" (Hanson 2005, 1297)—to gather information about who constitutes key family network members.

## The Diaspora Context

Since the mid-1970s, Ghana has experienced large scale, out migration, creating what has been termed a new diaspora. As noted in chapter 4, estimates suggest that 3 million Ghanaians live abroad (Anarfi et al. 2003), including 30 percent of all educated Ghanaians (*Economist* 2002, 38–40). Ghanaian migrants have relocated to neighboring West African countries and South Africa (Bump 2006), but the largest numbers have settled in Western European cities and eastern cities in North America. Ghanaians, like other diaspora groups, have developed networks rooted in clan/family as well as in hometown associations (HTAs) (although Ghanaian HTAs are neither as developed nor as institutionalized as Middle American HTAs in the United States) (Henry and Mohan 2003; Caglar 2006).

The political climate is welcoming for members of the diaspora. The current ruling New Patriotic Party (NPP) is making efforts to strengthen and institutionalize relationships with the diaspora community, aiming to harness capital for development purposes and encouraging Ghanaians abroad to return. A high-profile Ghana Homecoming Summit (attended by the president of Ghana, the entire cabinet, and a few thousand returnees) was held in 2001 to cement connections. The developmental impacts of this effort are unknown. Some Ghanaians from the diaspora believed the summit marked a benchmark for encouraging their national development input (Ghana Review 2001). Other members of the diaspora (Zachary 2005) have criticized the summit because government policy lacked real initiative for the productive deployment of returnees' funds. Both sides, however, concur that the summit only catered to the wealthy. Surprisingly, the summit did not target the Lebanese, a diaspora group noted for experience and success in raising funds so that they have been able to dominate parts of formal retail and import-export trade (Zachary 2005). Responding to some critics, the government recently turned their attention toward harnessing smaller funds from overseas Ghanaians. In March 2006, USAID-government of Ghana cosponsored "The Accra Regional Forum on Remittances and Trade in the West Africa Region" to rethink and improve the regulatory environment for small, informal financial transactions across borders (the sum of which is allegedly significant).

The government weaves a careful path between attracting investment, encouraging return migration, and giving a voice to the diaspora migrants, who potentially could be the wild card in local politics. Granting diaspora migrants a vote is still controversial in Ghana, as it is elsewhere.

The government introduced a Dual Citizenship Act in 2000 to cement these relationships, even though the act only offers a weak dual citizenship. Notwithstanding, the national rhetoric welcomes returnees and their investment funds.

There are numerous examples of diaspora members organizing to initiate development. Ashesi University, profiled in the introduction, is a good example of one project in the implementation stage. The GCG initiative (http://www.ghanacybergroup.com) is another effort that aims to build an Accra Technology Park, specializing in global outsourcing. Other projects under consideration (by the Ewe Association of Chicago) include investing in salt manufacturing and sporting goods manufacturing (Orozco 2005, 37). For the most part, however, investment efforts tend to be informal and smaller scale. Officials at GIPC emphasize that most foreign investments (in land, buildings, and small businesses) are made by individuals rather than firms, and individuals seldom register with the agency (Ghanaian law requires foreign investments to be registered with the GIPC).[2]

Reliable figures on the number of returnees and the value of returnees' investments are not available. Neither the Ghana Immigration Service nor the GIPC has the capacity to collect data on returnees' investments. The designation of a returnee migrant is problematic. Not all migrants register and/or unregister themselves, and return migrants with dual citizenship are extremely difficult to identify.

Return migrants to Ghana come home with more capital and education than they had on departure (Black, King and Litchfield 2003). Data from the Ghana Living Standards Survey (GSS 2003) indicate that approximately 50,000 migrants had returned to Ghana, and it is assumed that most returned from Europe and North America (Bump 2006, 10). We have no way of knowing how accurate this figure is; it does not count the number of returnees who come home informally/illegally. The number of Ghanaian returnees who use institutional programs is small (Black, King and Tiemoko 2003). For example, the German Office of Returnees provided assistance to "400 return migrants to Ghana" through the Ruckkehrburos (established in 1980) (Berkhout et al. 2005, 72). The program emphasized job placement in

2. Interview with Kwodwo Filson, deputy director, GIPC, June 7 2002.

healthcare, agriculture, and public administration and on good governance. However, self-assessments by program administrators have questioned the program's achievements; most returnees become entrepreneurs when the funding ended (Berkhout et al. 2005). Similarly the Dutch governments' Enterprising Across Borders program, established in 1998, provided assistance to only forty Ghanaian returnees (Berkhout et al. 2005).

## IDENTIFYING RETURNEES

I identified returnees from a household survey I conducted, and defined them as individuals who lived and worked in another country for at least one year. Subsequently, I selected returnees opportunistically for interviewing; eighteen were interviewed about their business and housing investments and regarding their networks. I recognize that return migrants' accounts of their own accomplishments are highly subjective and may overestimate their importance. I also acknowledge that my sample is biased, capturing the elite group who built new houses and remain in Accra without being forced to migrate further. As such, I cannot analyze returnees who came back with little or no capital and those who reside in Ghanaian-family homes/rental accommodations. However, my focus on the most successful returnees allows for assessing their contributions in a globalizing city.

## RETURNING "HOME"?

Sixty-eight heads of households surveyed were returnees. When I asked returnees why they moved back to Ghana, most emphasized opportunities in Accra rather than difficulties abroad as motivating factors. Forty percent mentioned a "fortuitous opportunity" (cash windfall, marriage, business partnership, house completion) that culminated in their return. One-third of returnees were enticed by investment opportunities. Ten percent reported that returning home was a chance to live in close proximity to relatives. Many were motivated to improve the quality of their lives by earning "more respect within society." Returnees' sense of respect was perceived to be elevated by a new centrality within family networks. Only a minority returned because they "had little choice": immigration issues, terminations of contracts, failures in getting established, and difficulties in living abroad (e.g., higher than expected expenses, racism, isolation, divorce, and "bad luck") were all mentioned.

Returnees were typically family units (the average unit comprised a head of household, a spouse, and two children). Frequently, the income earner stayed abroad to provide steady income flows to sustain the family and fund various business ventures. This arrangement seemed to satisfy both the nuclear family and the extended family; the migrant financially covered all of the costs of the nuclear family and provided assistance to the extended family (e.g., supporting individual family members, family business ventures, and covering for "hard times"). The high costs of repaying loans required some heads of households to continue earning abroad. Some business arrangements (e.g., exports between a European/North American group and an affiliate in Ghana) necessitated the coordination of activities abroad to ensure face-to-face contact with suppliers. Often, a nuclear family member liaised with extended family members on behalf of the head of the household so he or she could concentrate all of his or her energies on earning. Certainly, operating "bootstrap enterprises" with limited funds and no experience encouraged this trend.

My research uncovered two groups of returnees: elites and nonelites. Elites invested in the upper end of the housing market in expensive gated communities and in lump sums often over US$121,000 (reflecting market prices for houses and private developers' payment schedules). Other elites made continuous small housing investments into new builder areas. Their combined investments ranged between US$11,000 and US$80,000. Nonelites invested around US$10,000, mainly in traditional areas where they built on family properties (Table 5.1). Some nonelites also built in individual builder areas. Many invested in plots they acquired before land became expensive.

About one-quarter of the elite group was differentiated by their capacity to continue remitting from abroad (through investments they held onto or from the foreign component of local business enterprises and pension funds) even though they regarded their move to Accra as permanent. Nonelites also received remittances but less regularly, and these funds were used for survival rather than investment. About a third of returnees (mostly elites

TABLE 5.1

NEW HOUSING INVESTMENT BY COST

| | |
|---|---|
| Under US$10,000 | 19 |
| US$11,000–40,000 | 10 |
| US$41,000–80,000 | 4 |
| US$81,000–120,000 | 14 |
| >US$121,000 | 21 |
| Total | 68 |

*Source:* Grant 2004.

but also some nonelites) managed to keep some foreign currency abroad, hedging against the devaluation of the cedi as well as keeping options open. Returnees with dual citizenships moved with ease and had reliable access to foreign-held funds through Internet banking/financial companies.

Incremental investing allowed for building capital and for testing the waters prior to return. Investments sent from abroad enabled migrants to develop their own institutions, notably festive kin networks that served as risk-reducing mechanisms. Sending money back home and investing in family plots and/or small projects, such as buying a taxi, were viewed as valuable opportunities to test the business environment, to gauge profitability, and to observe how festive kin behaved with money. Many derived benefits from this; profits accrued and important relationships with family and friends were solidified.

There was a considerable range in returnees' current employment (Table 5.2). Fifteen percent were employed by foreign companies. Another fifteen percent were retirees. One-half of returnees were self-employed in small businesses in the service and trade sector. Returnee enterprises included consulting, financial services, advertising, medical service clinics, real estate service, restaurants, import-export, retail, education, business, and personal services. Many self-employed returnees operated companies as the sole owner, and worked as independent consultants, retailers, import-exporters, builders, courier/drivers, tour operators, journalists, and artisans. Some of these operations had links abroad, but foreign travel was rare.

Approximately one-third of all returnees operated as transnational entrepreneurs (i.e., a business investor abroad was affiliated with Accra

TABLE 5.2

EMPLOYMENT OF RETURNEES

| Nature of employment | Percentage* |
|---|---|
| Foreign company | 15 |
| Domestic company | 6 |
| Retiree | 15 |
| Unemployed | 6 |
| Refusals | 3 |
| Unspecified business interests | 6 |
| Self-employed | 50 |

*Source:* Grant 2004; interviews.
 *Percentages do not add up to 100% because of rounding.

entrepreneurial activity, and related business involved traveling abroad at least twice a year). Transnational entrepreneurs represent a sizable group among returnees. Typically, transnational entrepreneurs conducted business with their former host country/countries. A few identified new countries with which they dealt, but noted that a family member was now living there. Most commonly, the transnational network was used either to supply goods in import-export trade or for client referrals to service sector activities. The geography of transnational enterprise connections appears similar to the dominant migration patterns identified (Bump 2006) (Table 5.3).

Additional examples of transnational businesses include consultancies that depend on offices abroad (in the UK, the United States, Canada, and Lebanon) to secure contract work, and there were various import operations that depend on family members abroad (in Europe, North America, and Lebanon) to run the foreign arm of the business venture. Some self-employed individuals depended on business operations abroad for their employment; for example, there were courier service companies that delivered money and packages from Accra to Nigeria and Togo. There were also examples of returnees contracted by companies outside of Ghana. For example, a self-employed truck driver, contracted by a company in Burkina Faso/Niger, made pickups at Tema Port and deliveries throughout West Africa.

Despite success stories, interviews with returnees revealed failures and pointed to family obstacles. Many returnees revealed painful experiences of

TABLE 5.3

TRANSNATIONAL ENTREPRENEURS

| Transnational enterprises | Business locations |
| --- | --- |
| Import-export (cars) | Netherlands, Germany, United Kingdom-Accra |
| Import-export (clothing) | United States, United Kingdom, France-Accra |
| Import-export (food stuffs) | Nigeria, Lebanon, Europe-Accra |
| Import-export (building materials) | Germany, United Kingdom-Accra |
| Import-export (business machinery) | United Kingdom-Nigeria,-Accra |
| Real estate development | United States, United Kingdom, Italy, Netherlands, Canada-Accra |
| Investor | United States, Europe-Accra |
| Real estate | United States-Europe-Accra |
| Medical clinic | United States-United Kingdom-Accra |
| Consulting firm | United Kingdom, United States, Canada, Lebanon-Accra |
| Construction firm | Germany, United Kingdom-Accra |
| Courier/driver | Burkina Faso, Niger, Nigeria, Togo, Benin, Cote d'Ivoire-Accra |

*Source:* Grant 2004; interviews.

money evaporating and funds squandered by trusted partners who, in turn, relied on untrustworthy local associates. A few reported being cheated by friends and family. One interviewee detailed the mishandling of his investments.[3] Friends and relatives misspent US$5,000 in purchasing substandard equipment to furnish a communication center and made deals to pay premium rent for the premises. When the interviewee became aware that the estate agent was a cousin of the friend entrusted to take charge of the project, it became apparent that the local network had conspired to usurp most of funds and they had tried to cover their tracks. Overall, it seems that reconnecting by investing produced both good and bad experiences. Nevertheless, most emphasized their commitment to return and to get things done with festive kin support.

Once they returned, individuals engaged in networking. Returning entailed making the rounds so that people realized individuals have come

---

3. Interview with returnee "Samuel" who wished to remain anonymous, May 15, 2005.

home for good. It always involved opening local bank accounts. As a result, returnees have much higher participation rates in banking than the general Ghanaian population: 100 percent compared to 5 percent for Ghanaian average (*Ghanaian Chronicle* 2004). Considerable efforts were put into establishing new networks. Elites joined tennis and golf clubs; organizations that represented new initiatives for expanding networks. For instance, the tennis and pool facilities at the Golden Tulip Hotel in Accra received frequent mentions as the important returnee node for cementing new relationships. Nonelites reported spending time with relatives and friends and making considerable efforts to get to know people in their neighborhood. Many joined professional organizations or local chapters. A few mentioned intentions to get involved in the local arm of HTAs.

RETURNEE NETWORKS

I conducted eighteen interviews with returnees to shed light on the geography of their networks. I asked about their family network, the network around their house, their neighborhood network, and their entrepreneurial network. I used these interviews to obtain an overall sense of the depth, size, and reach of networks. I asked returnees who provided them assistance in setting up once they returned and who they counted on in an emergency. For the most part, networking was both strategic and calculative; returnees participated in networking to improve economic and social mobility (See also Hanson 2005).

Each interviewee articulated a unique network but I discerned two general tracks: one for those with smaller investments and another for those with larger investments. Figures 5.1 and 5.2 provide an illustration of the social fields of both low- and higher-income transnational entrepreneurs. They summarize the average number of contact points for both cohorts in each social field, identify overlaps, and reveal the extent to which contact points are situated in local or international fields. Network membership was about the same as Hanson found for nationally based networks (eight key pivots on average for each network). There are obvious limits to the total number of pivotal relationships individuals can reasonably maintain.

There were a number of commonalities to both upper- and lower-income networks. Individuals maintained approximately eight contact people per

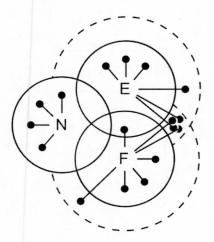

Figure 5.1. Morphology of an Upper-Income Transnational Entrepreneur. Source: Grant 2004; interviews.

network (with the exception of upper-income residents, who, on average, have four contact points per neighborhood). Family and business enterprise networks were central to both cohorts. The central difference for return networks was two or three active contact points in the network outside of Ghana. This provides evidence of "the double engagement" returnees are able to maintain. I need to underscore that Ghanaians abroad account for half of the key contacts abroad. Depending on individual circumstances (occupation, whether the spouse was Ghanaian or not, the length of time spent abroad, etc.), interviewees emphasized key contacts within an inner

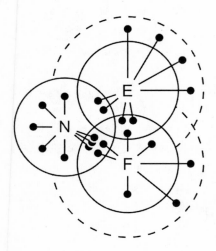

Figure 5.2. Morphology of a Lower-Income Transnational Entrepreneur. Source: Grant 2004; interviews.

social circle of friends, colleagues, and business partners living abroad whom they relied on and trusted. Networks were interlocking, both domestically and internationally. Interviewees held a geographical construction of the domestic versus the international and assigned individuals in networks to one of the two realms. Some active contacts moved back and forth between the two realms. For instance, several respondents identified family members living abroad and represented them as both foreign business partners and local family members. The frequency of family members' travel back and forth to Accra allowed this duality.

## FAMILY-KIN NETWORKS: A VIEW FROM THE NEW HOUSE

New house purchases have almost become a competition among migrants, and a topic of gossip and comparison among returnees and festive kin. Returnees mostly paid for the costs of new houses from savings earned abroad; family loans and remittances contributed much lesser funds. Few returnees secured mortgages from Ghanaian banks. Most returnees owned a separate house for the nuclear family, distinct from the Ghanaian-family house. Their accumulated wealth and exposure to Western lifestyles, emphasizing individualism, explains this trend. Desire for a level of privacy similar to that experienced abroad, and that which cannot be expected in the Ghanaian-family home, was also a significant factor. Privacy also extended to business arrangements. Because some returnees engaged in entrepreneurial activities at home as well as abroad, they needed to keep the details of business arrangements "in-house." If the spouse is non-Ghanaian and/or the children were initially raised abroad before returning, a separate house was an important consideration.

Most explained their preference of returning to Accra rather than opting to live elsewhere in Ghana (hometowns and/or other more affordable locations). Returnees claimed that the more prestigious locations in hometowns had already been acquired and they did not want a property on the periphery of rural towns that had already been littered with spacious houses, many of which were financed by migrants who still lived abroad.

Many interviewees expressed the dual responsibility of building two houses but articulated the desirability to separate the nuclear and the extended family homes. As one interviewee noted, "Yes, it costs a lot to build two houses. I built my own house in a private gated community and then one for the family in our home village. I was obliged to do it because it was like a social investment but it made little economic sense. You do not get any respect unless you can be located within various circles. The local family wanted to have a house in the village and that is important to them. For my business and international friends, it is important that I live in a prestigious community that is well connected to the larger world."[4]

However, it was also common for the new nuclear family house to serve as the urban node in family networks that extended overseas (whereby packages, mail, messages, and sometimes e-mail could be received and transmitted). Some fulfilled family financial obligations by allowing family members to operate small businesses from the nuclear family property (kiosks for petty trade and Internet-related businesses, for example). As mentioned in the previous chapter, investing in a new expensive house sent a signal about their resources and commitment to the Ghanaian family. Returnees in particular were adamant that housing investments indirectly benefitted the extended family's position, in particular its access to informal credit. Returnees' fixed presence in the community (as opposed to nonresident Ghanians) appeared to serve as a guarantee of sorts. Two returnees even claimed that their housing investments enabled extended family members to realize benefits in the marriage market.[5]

Most interviewees acknowledged a politics of inclusion over who was welcome to live under the roof as a nonpaying guest. About half of the interviewees mentioned that from time to time they accommodated family members abroad traveling to Ghana, but conspicuously absent were mentions of nontraveling extended family members. (Supposedly these family members had already settled in other locations.) Many interviewees emphasized that the migration-and-return process also initiated social transformation within the extended family.

Returnees regarded themselves as central network coordinators. Because they had acquired capital and international experience, returnees emphasized

4. Interview with returnee "Kofi" who wished to remained anonymous, May 14, 2005.

5. Interview with returnee "Victoria" who wished to remain anonymous, July 9, 2005.

repeatedly that the Ghanaian family was very sensitive to their complex existence, and that they assumed a vital pivotal role in linking family in Ghana
and family overseas. Sometimes this involved assuming advisory roles for
many family members; for example, helping to reduce conflict and getting
those abroad to share in financial responsibilities. As one interviewee put it,
"I have become respected by all family members, those who live in Ghana
and those who live in the United States and Holland. I broker everyone's
world, and I am trusted by all because I understand how things are here and
how things are *not* over there."[6] She explained her considerable efforts in
persuading extended family members "not to expect too much and not to be
disappointed when money comes late and it is very small."[7]

As mentioned above, visiting nuclear family members from abroad were
always welcomed at the house. These family members were the source of
financial injections and they brought euros and dollars for the payment of
association fees, house repairs, additions and improvements, and various
consumer and luxury items (e.g., electronics). Visiting family members also
assisted in keeping international networks vibrant so returnees could maintain a foothold in several countries simultaneously.

NEIGHBORHOOD NETWORK: A VIEW FROM THE NEW HOUSE

In Accra, the neighborhood has traditionally been viewed as a pivotal arena
for cementing festive kin relationships. The large share of dwelling units classified as compound housing reinforced this aspect of a society where contact,
mutual reliance, exchanges of favors, and assistance were central to daily life.
Physical and sociocultural proximity supported these relationships, supporting the neighborhood network. Virtually all returnees with new housing
investments did not build a compound house; instead they mainly opted for
single-family dwelling units, most often western-style villas.

I uncovered very different experiences in returnee efforts to redefine and
separate social spaces. Returnees with housing investments under US$10,000
chose to live in residential areas where some family members resided. The

---

6. Interview with "Liz" who wished to remain anonymous, July 9, 2005.
7. Interview with returnee "Emmanuel" who wished to remain anonymous, July 3, 2005.

process of acquiring plots and building from abroad meant they entrusted family networks that, in turn, had familiarity and contacts in particular areas. Some identified proximity to relatives, and more specifically the benefits of raising children with family in the vicinity, as the prime locational decision-making factor. For the most part, returnees with housing investments over US$40,000 went back neither to their former residential locations nor to locations where current family members reside. Elites with investments around US$121,000 opted to live in new private and gated communities. A striking aspect to these residential areas was the smaller number of active contacts within the neighborhood (Fig 5.2). Perhaps, the fact that private and gated communities are newer neighborhoods still in a formative stage might explain much of this trend. In addition, living in gated communities meant a complete separation from the extended family. For some, living in gated communities presented opportunities for establishing business and social contacts. However, in general, weak residential community involvement and few active neighbor contacts was the norm. This finding calls into question the development of a real community within the newer and expensive private residential developments. This finding is in sharp contrast with lower-income residents, who develop more contacts in their neighborhood, and family networks in the neighborhood overlapped in many instances, no doubt facilitating the development of active contacts after the return.

Because most returnees with housing investment live in new residential areas, there is a different residential politics of inclusion than found in traditional residential areas. Developing meaningful relationships takes time in a new neighborhood. However, returnees emphasized that they had established networks when they lived abroad, so establishing networks with neighbors was, in theory, less complicated, but in reality, very slow. It seemed that returnees found it easier to establish relationships with other returnees in their neighborhood. Absentee owners (common in private estates) were networking barriers. Many homeowners distinguished between owners and renters in their neighborhood. Many noted that they did not want to spend energy connecting with caretakers, homeowners' relatives, and/or renters unless they were immediate neighbors. Nonowners were viewed as cordial but not as active contacts. Housing investors appeared to exhibit a detailed knowledge of owners and others in their residential area. Resident associations were reported as important opportunities for cultivating social relationships and for working on neighborhood issues (planning), which helped formed solid friendships among the most active members. However, many returnees were not active in the residential association.

## ENTREPRENEURIAL NETWORKS

Three-quarters of returnees reported nonlinear careers, revealing a significant difference in their current and former occupations abroad. Only seven returnees received official assistance and program support (two received private bank support, four were supported by German and Dutch development programs, and one was supported by a USAID program). No returnees obtained financial support from the government of Ghana. Returnees expressed distrust of governmental programs, noting that failed state policies were one of most important push factors in initial migration decision making. Some interviewees were critical of government programs, portraying them as "bureaucratic," "slow," "inept," and "irrelevant to making it in a global economy."[8] There were some who reported more positive experiences related to governmental programs and specifically to the mentoring they obtained from officials at the GIPC and the Private Enterprise Foundation.[9]

For the most part, returnees who were interviewed emphasized their desire to guard their business ideas or models; fearing leaks might undermine their potential for success. Many highlighted that they had to move forward, hit the ground running, and deploy their accumulated savings. Most commonly, returnees implemented entrepreneurial initiatives after obtaining housing. One-quarter of returnees (mostly higher skilled) established the foreign component of business operations before returning and completed the entrepreneurial network locally. Many emphasized that they sought a hands-on approach to all aspects of their business venture. Some highly skilled returnees noted that by becoming citizens in another land (e.g., the United States or Europe), they had enhanced their business prospects back

8. Interview with returnee "Kojo" who wished to remain anonymous, July 12, 2005.
9. Ibid.

home because they had the freedom to travel and the credentials to obtain business loans when needed. It was more common for lower-skilled returnees to have a number of business ideas and to go about ascertaining the feasibility (informally) of different initiatives before launching an effort. Some also mentioned that they tried a number of initiatives before they embarked on their current project.

I previously mentioned efforts to keep business investments private but for the most part, returnees selectively employed festive kin members. Important decisions about who to involve or exclude had to be made. Many minimized the risks and expenses by employing relatives and friends and by working through their networks. A selective involvement of festive kin members was a consistent element in most bootstrap enterprises. As one interviewee put it "you learn that when it comes to money some family members change and cannot be trusted but others show loyalty and see and appreciate the benefits."[10] A number of returnees did not establish their own business but rather took on organizing roles in the development of an immediate family member's own business. Besides financing these ventures, returnees assumed facilitating roles, often extending their networks' abroad.

It was highlighted time and again that festive kin encouraged returnees to start businesses in Accra rather than in hometowns or alternative locations, and family members were more than willing to relocate to Accra (from elsewhere in Ghana) to participate fully in entrepreneurial activities. Many interviewees revealed that difficult decisions had to be made about the people to involve and what tasks to assign to particular individuals. Many reported consulting family members for advice but emphasized that they themselves made the final decisions. It was clear in many cases that key positions were assigned to close relatives (children, brothers, sisters, so forth) and less important or part-time duties were often shared among the children of festive kin. No doubt the advice given to returnees reflected at least in part the business ambitions of locals and their positioning for inclusion. Overall, the net result of involving family members in entrepreneurial activities helped solidify Accra's centrality not only in entrepreneurial space but also in family space.

10. Interview with returnee "Kofi" who wished to remain anonymous, May 14, 2005.

CONCLUSIONS

Clearly returnees are making an impact on economic development in Accra. Overall, they account for considerable housing investments and are responsible for starting a wide variety of bootstrap enterprises. Their investments into the housing sector are easier to quantify than their enterprises, which is ironic given that the housing/land sector operates under a traditional system. The sample of sixty-eight returnees invested US$523,000 million in the housing market. Returnees had high participation rates in the urban economy, securing employment in foreign and domestic companies as well as operating thirty-four business enterprises. There is some evidence that high levels of returnee participation might represent a new episode in the development paradigm (Ammassari 2004). However, much more extensive research is needed to document the cumulative investments of returnees' businesses and to ascertain business profitability, failures, and contributions to employment compared to other groups in the urban economy.

In terms of the lives returnees reestablished back home, there are politics of inclusion in living arrangements, neighborhood, and business networks. Certainly this reality is no different than many households around the world. But in the Ghanaian cultural context, it represents a break from traditional lifestyles and a movement toward nuclear family units; nuclear investment portfolios. Accra returnees are weaving in-between networks that are entangling more and more people into transnational space.

Not all returnees were successful in their investments in Ghana. Some returnees reported that their ventures had failed. Many bought plots and paid for housing that never materialized. Some credited business failure to their lack of capital and/or management experience. Some were adamant that the Accra environment was very competitive for start-ups; many individuals independently came up with similar and rival businesses. A few suggested that it was too difficult to combine a foreign and a local business, that their return stuck them "in between" with little control over individuals abroad and too much reliance on locals. Others felt themselves to be unlucky and wanted to return to the United States or Europe but hoped to be able to maintain their Accra housing investment, which they regarded as a sound investment.

The morphology of returnee networks was highly varied, but some generalizations can be made. The networks of both groups of transnational entrepreneurs showed that individuals used active contacts both at home and abroad to pursue business initiatives. For these individuals, return migration combined maintaining links abroad in order for them to stay at home. More important, it represented a new "double engagement."

There is a pressing need for further research on many aspects of return migrants' networks (Ammassari 2005). For instance, are the networks within the country used benevolently or exploitatively? It is far from clear whether inherent class differentiation allows the wealthy or "wordly" to extract labor from the festive kin or whether the festive kin are able to extract resources from returnees because of their position within the traditional society. We know little about the development of returnees' social networks, and how those are viewed by extended family members, local business associates, neighborhood associations, etc. The larger migration question of what effects the perceived successes of returnees' bootstrap enterprises have on encouraging future migration streams to acquire capital is unknown. The extent to which returnees are successful in securing their own housing in an environment where most are destined to rent is important to understand.

# 6

# Globalizing from Below

*Slum Dwellers in a Globalizing City*

IN THE CONTEXT OF PROTRACTED DEBATES about informal set-
tler evictions in Accra, four slum dwellers, supported by a local NGO leader,
obtained passports, purchased airline tickets, and participated in a Nairobi
"official" visit. The slum dwellers had never traveled outside of Ghana before.
In Nairobi, the four slum dwellers received a delegations' welcome. There,
they met with municipal officials and representatives from community based
organizations, traveled to Kibera (one of the largest slums in Africa), and
held face-to-face meetings with local slum dwellers. During their exposure
trip, they discussed community organization and urban rehabilitation efforts,
among other things. The government of Ghana did not arrange the Accra-
Nairobi visit. Instead, a local community organization, with links to an international nongovernmental organization, strategically planned the visit.

A requirement for participation in the Nairobi exposure trip was that
slum dwellers had to keep diaries and record their observations and self-
reflections. One member of the delegation expressed that "the Nairobi
exchange is the emergence of a new era that links Accra's settlers with communities on the other side of the continent."[1] He went on to reflect that he
"is getting firsthand knowledge and experience . . . and knows that (informal) settlers in Accra will have a future." The Nairobi visit, combined with
a series of other NGO-initiated events in Accra, such as the Old Fadama
slum receiving a visit from South African slum organizers, illustrates the

1. Interview with Old Fatima representative who wishes to remain anonymous, May 10,
2005.

very different backdrop to the usual politics surrounding the future of urban slums in Africa.

All of these actions were taken because rapid rates of urbanization in Accra have put new pressures on land and its value (Berry 2000; Mabogunje 1992; Juul and Lund 2002) and called for new thinking. I contend that a new political geography of landlessness and homelessness is emerging in globalizing Accra on a scale not witnessed before. The poor's desire for survival means they cannot operate in the typical political sphere. Their survival calls for action at different scales that were previously unthinkable. NGO-initiated intervention encourages the poor to frame their situation in a global context. Movements among the urban poor, such as the branch I document in Accra are connected to Shack/Slum Dwellers International (SDI).[2] SDI involves an international federation spanning twenty-one countries in 2008 whose members share ideas and experiences and lend each other support in their efforts to secure access to housing, infrastructure, and land (D'Cruz and Mitlin 2004).

A transformation is underway; local squatters are transitioning toward active globalizing citizens. Three developments have facilitated this trend. First, there is a new importance of a different politics of scale in urban land. The presence of an NGO (that otherwise would not have been there) in a particular place can connect that place into a global network and bring new meanings, resources, forms of power, and a range of other influences to bear on that place (Bebbington 2004, 732). Accordingly, the choice of spatial scale is not one or another but possibly both or more, entailing inherent complexities. The most politically successful grassroots organizations become part of a geographically flexible network in which there is an intermingling of the scales of political action to the extent that the scales can become mutually constitutive (Routledge 2003).

2. SDI is a network organization with a presence in South Asia, Africa, and Latin America. It grew out of alliances formed in the mid-1980s by three Indian organizations: the National Slum Dwellers Federation, Mahila Milan (a network of poor women), and the Society for the Promotion of Area Resource Centers (a research group). International networking led to the development of a similar approach comprising parallel organizations and peoples in South Africa, Namibia, and Zimbabwe (Huchzermeyer 2004, 73).

Second, NGOs and citizens' movements are appropriating urban governance functions (Appadurai 2001; Taylor 2005). New forms of globally organized power and expertise operate inside national boundaries (Ranney 2003), but elites are not the only ones who can harness global expertise to design policies and to position their interests in the national and urban economies. At the same time, interventions in housing for the urban poor do not have to be dependent on the World Bank and/or national governments anymore (Huchzermeyer 2004). DeFillippis (2004, 35) emphasizes that these new relationships connecting particular places with the rest of the world have the capacity to generate new urban politics, create new localities, and make new social meanings in the process.

Third, new political horizons are being shaped when members of the poor pursue cross-border activism (Appadurai 2001). On the ground, this means that individuals are taking independent action ahead of national government policy and sometimes in direct opposition to local political elites. Various groups are attempting to pressure the state to take a specific course of action or to adopt a new specific policy (Tostensen et al. 2001). In many ways, the emerging global discourse on reducing poverty in Africa is providing a powerful boost to particular emerging civil society formations. Ghana is signature to the Millennium Developmental goals, which means issues about housing, shelter, and strategies to reduce poverty have a current salience and visibility. The poor can now not only be seen but also be heard.

In this chapter, I argue that rather than viewing informal settlements as marginalized and excluded spaces, the poorest of the poor can also act as globalizing agents. I contend that slum communities and squatter settlements are neither defeated nor disorganized (Perlman 1976). Just as global command functions are often highly localized (Taylor 2005), slum connections, although rooted in a specific local context, have potential to crisscross the globe. I use a case study of the Agbogbloshie/Old Fadama settlement (the most controversial slum in Accra) to highlight efforts of globalization from below. I document how the main stakeholders in the area emphasize new relationships and routinely jump scales (utilizing international expertise and global connections) to justify positions on land claims.

GLOBALIZING CITY: THE NEW INFORMAL CITYSCAPE

Despite informal housing and spontaneous settlements constituting a major part of the residential geographies in African cities, squatter settlements were rare in urban West Africa before 1990 (Konadu-Agyemang 1991; Peil 1976). The United Nations Human Settlements Programme (2003, xxv) calculates that 924 million, or 31.6 percent of the world's population, live in slums, and a good proportion of these are classified as squatter settlements.

According to Konadu-Agyemang (1991, 140), "cities in [western] Anglophone Africa, although characterized by all the conditions, which have led to the development of squatter settlements elsewhere, are relatively free from such settlements." Their absence was explained by the land tenure system, which makes access to land easy, government intervention in the housing market as a provider of low-income housing, and peoples' attitudes to land, which are shaped by traditional beliefs, religious myths, and taboos. Cultural factors that privileged the chiefs as the custodians of land shaped the political environment (Tipple et al. 1997). Urban chiefs wielded considerable power over urban migrants because migrants typically lived under the influence of chiefs in their rural homes, and being landowners in their own right through communal holdings, they knew that squatting on someone else's land provoked serious trouble. This safeguard, combined with beliefs about the superintending role of the spirits (hovering around the properties of their families and capable of bringing harm to those who might wrongfully or unjustifiably occupy this land), meant land was protected (Konadu-Agyemang 1991). In addition, affordable land and accommodations or both were available. Plots of land were available at nominal costs for occupation. Before 1990, about one-quarter of urban residents lived rent-free in Ghana (Korboe 1992, 1159). The Accra land environment had enormous absorption capacity. For instance, 1 million Ghanaians were repatriated from Nigeria in 1983 without creating large squatter settlements.

Slums and squatter settlements are now widespread in Accra. Mike Davis' (2006, 6) *Planet of Slums* considers an extensive slum constellation comprising of the entire area along the Accra corridor (stretching from Accra to Benin City) "the biggest single footprint of poverty on earth." Davis's (2006) characterization exaggerates the prevalence of slums but there is virtually no data on Accra slums. The 2000 Population and Housing Census provide some clues to the growth as well as the spread of slums in Accra. Map 6.1 shows the geography of nonpermanent dwellings in Accra. It is important to sketch the scale of informality in Accra because it illustrates the wider context in which debates about shelter emerge (Hansen and Vaa 2004). The ubiquitous geography of nonpermanent dwellings is the other side of the residential geography of a globalizing city.

Most residential areas are peppered with nonpermanent dwellings (most of which are erected without permits and/or planning approval). Within residential areas, there are significant variations on the ground, varying block by block, street by street, and land parcel by land parcel.

The geography of informality has five features. First, there is the development of large slum/squatter areas (Agbogbloshie/Old Fadama, Ashaiman, etc.) that have emerged to provide affordable accommodation for migrants and other urbanites. These areas provide a reserve of cheap labor for sectors such as food and informal construction. Second, there are areas where housing conditions have severely deteriorated (e.g., Nima, Labadi, Sabon Zongo). More crowding in these areas coupled with residents being tighter squeezed economically has resulted in a different type of building boom:

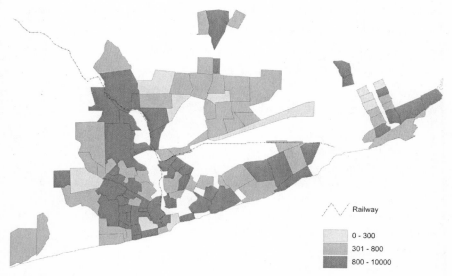

Map 6.1. Residential Geography of Informal Structures in 2000. Source: GSS 2004.

adding rooms/kiosks and shops incrementally for renting. Third, there are kiosks and semipermanent front and backyard workshops that dot upscale residential areas like Legon and Airport. Individuals have been pushed to add on informally so they can survive economically and/or assist in fulfilling extended family obligations by allowing relatives to live cheaply and/or run a microenterprise adjacent to the owner's property. Fourth, there are temporary workshops, primarily serving the residential construction industry (block making, sand and stone winning, machine repairs, etc.), that often relocate in time in accordance with the shifting contours of residential building. Fifth, there are microenterprises in services and production that have sprung up everywhere, and cluster heavily along major thoroughfares, in road reservations, and on idle parcels of land.

This chapter details the first, and most worrying trend—slum and squatter formation. I detail the evolution of the most controversial land issue in Accra, the Korle Lagoon environs, to illustrate how slum and squatter settlers engage internationally.

## LAND HISTORY OF KORLE LAGOON AREA AND THE EVOLUTION OF A SQUATTER SETTLEMENT

The land of Agbogbloshie/Old Fadama is 146.21 hectares. It is a triangle of land bounded by the Abossey Okai Road, the Odaw River (in the upper reaches of the Korle Lagoon) and the Agbogbloshie Drain, less than a kilometer from Accra's CBD (Map 6.2).

The population could be as high as 40,000.[3] Living conditions are poor and characterized by high-density living in wooden shacks and kiosks. There

3. There are no current accurate surveys or statistics on the occupied parts of the lagoon. The GSS puts the counted population at 4,505 and other sources estimate 30,000 (COHRE 2004). Local community leaders explain the large discrepancy by noting the significant differences between day and night population numbers. The population rises at night as many workers come back to sleep from informal sector activities. At night, some rooms sleep up to twenty renters. Moreover, about 10,000 people are reported to be temporary residents, many of whom come from the north for short-term work as head-carriers (kayoyou) at local markets. Once these individuals obtain enough savings for a wedding or small business, they return to their villages. Because this portion of the population is always in flux it makes an accurate census difficult.

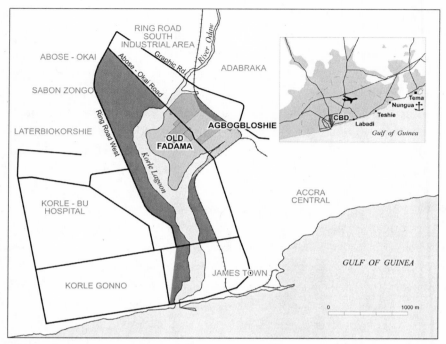

Map 6.2. Korle Lagoon Within the Accra Metropolitan Context. Source: Grant 2006.

are no sanitary facilities and all kinds of waste end up in the lagoon. The area is subject to frequent flooding in most parts of the year (and acute flooding in the rainy season), and is composed of two related human settlements with different origins.

First, there is the Agbogbloshie[4] formal settlement that has been surrounded by informal residential developments. The poorest squatters are along the railway line on the edge of the settlement. Agbogbloshie has a large commercial function and contains a number of food markets (namely the Makola Agbogbloshie food market), a commercial bus depot, numerous small shops and stalls, and a significant number of large industrial enterprises (e.g., brewing, paint manufacturing, engineering). In addition, the area contains a number of municipal authority offices (e.g., AMA market office) as

4. Agbogbloshie is a Ga traditional name for the area, and the name is associated with the Agboglo shrine located in the area.

well as a government tax collection office (e.g., IRS). Local leaders estimate that 15,000 people live in the area.[5] A good number of residents have titles to the lands they occupy; a few elders have titles from 1943. The land is now public, but in the past it was under the control of local stools, principally the Korle and Gbese stools.

The second settlement, Old Fadama, is an informal settlement located next to Agbogbloshie. It has a mix of commercial and residential functions, contains a large number of niche food markets (e.g., those specializing in yams, onions, tomatoes, etc.), a number of hawker markets, a variety of small economic enterprises, and services for residents (hairdressing, food production, dressmaking, etc.). A settlement profile conducted by local leadership put the total number of residents at 24,165,[6] but local community leaders estimate the current number to be closer to 35,000. The residents do not have title to the land they occupy, and the land is under control of the state.

Politics over land in the Agbogbloshie/Old Fadama area has deep roots. Three political time frames with specific historical roots are relevant to current land politics: 1. a period when traditional claims to the land clashed with colonial plans, 2. a period where the government acquired that land over traditional claims, and 3. the contemporary period, which has pitted the government against the settlers.

Historians (e.g., Parker 2000) have documented political controversy about this area during the colonial period. The politics revolved around the designation of the Korle Lagoon as sacred by the local traditional group, the Ga. In the opening and closing seasons of the lagoon for fishing, Ga traditional priests performed rituals honoring the body of water as a provider of individuals' livelihoods (Okeh 1957, 142). As a result, colonial town planning had limited intervention in this area. Land was acquired for a railway station in 1914 and for a village site,[7] but more urban development plans

5. Interview with Bampoe Addo, leader of first savings federation in Agbogbloshie, May 10, 2005.

6. The settlement profile was conducted on December 31, 2004 by the Old Fatima branch of the GHPF.

7. Deeds Registry no. 522/1914. Certificate of Title 24 September 1914 (Railway Station Site/East Agbogbloshie Village).

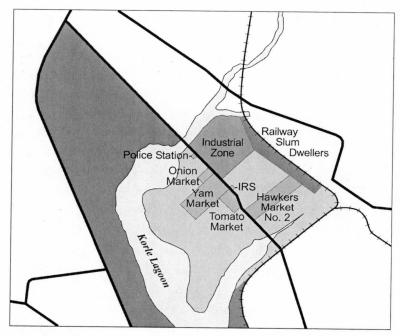

Map 6.3. Old Fadama and Agbogbloshie Settlements. Source: Grant 2006

clashed with Ga notions of ritual space. The political struggle over this land came to a head in 1920 when a British consortium approached town leadership requesting to lease the lagoon for conversion into harbor facilities. This proposal led to an intense political struggle, and local opposition became very vocal about "selling" the sacred lagoon to the Europeans. Colonial town planners then concentrated on the development of low-income housing estates beyond the area (at Korle Gonna, Sabon Zongo, etc.), developing "model" settlements for low-income residents that could be resettled from overcrowded CBD areas like Jamestown (Acquah 1957, 28). Two small low-income "village settlements" at Agbogbloshie and Fadama (with 298 houses) were identified in the 1952 Land Use Map (Acquah 1957, 168, fig. 6.9). Agbogloshie was composed of Ga, who had obtained land rights from the local chief (Accra Studio 2003). Fadama was composed of migrants who came from the Northern Ghana (Jack and Braimah 2004, 23). But for the most part, the lagoon remained in its natural state up to 1961 and supported "a thriving fishery of both fin and shellfish, which served as a source of employment of some people in nearby low income housing areas" (Boadi and Kuitunen 2002, 301).

In the second political frame, the government became directly involved in the area in 1961 when it claimed the land at "Accra-Fadama for Korle Lagoon Development" by issuing a Certificate of Title to the area.[8] Under the auspices of this intervention, land acquired in the public interest for development purposes extinguished all subsisting rights and interest to the lands. Subsequently, under the authority of the Accra Industrial Estate (Acquisition of Lands) Ordinance no. 28 (1956), land in the vicinity was allocated for a variety of industrial projects (brewing, food processing, and later auto repairs) (Accra Studio 2003, 132). In 1966 the government undertook a soil dredging exercise to reclaim land and raise the level of some of the flooded area along the Odaw River, including Agbogbloshie.[9] Some of the reclaimed lands were allocated for use by the government (State Housing Corporation, State Transport Corporation) as well as by light industry. The area of Old Fadama was left unused. Reclaiming efforts led to additional lands being added to the area, and failure to develop up-to-date maps of the area meant the boundaries became murky over time. Relevant compensation was reported to have been paid at the time of acquisition to the Korle and Gbese stools (Accra Studio 2003, 132). The Ga Traditional Council, an organization with authority to speak on behalf of the chiefs, has not disputed the government's right to use the land in the national interest for Korle Lagoon development.[10] The stool has maintained that in the event the land is not used for the intended purposes, the local stools will have a renewed claim to the land.

The government renewed restoration efforts with a development project known as the Korle Lagoon Ecological Restoration Project (KLERP) in the early 1990s. The government's explicit aim was to "restore the lagoon to its natural ecology and realign the lagoon to improve its hydrological efficiency to increase the flow of the water through the lagoon, and finally to develop

8. The Certificate of Title highlights lagoon development but also mentions acquisition for the purpose of locating a police reserve barracks and buildings for the Department of Agriculture. This land acquisition pertained to 361.29 acres of land (GOG 1961).

9. Executive Instrument 160/1966 Accra Korle Lagoon Project (Odaw Channel).

10. Interview with Gbese stool, May 12, 2005.

it into a major tourist attraction" (quoted in Boadi and Kuitunen 2002, 308). Funding for $73 million was secured for phase one of the restoration in 1999 from various sources (OPEC Fund for International Development, the Arab Bank for Economic Development in Africa, the Kuwait Fund for Arab Development). Restoration started in March 2000 and concentrated on dredging and removal of materials. A second phase began in 2003 and targeted "upgrading." A total of $48 million was raised from two sources: the Belgian government and a government loan from the Standard and Charter Bank of London. Upgrading in this context implies improving physical infrastructure (seawalls, drainage improvements), beautification of the lagoon (landscaping), and management (waste).

The arrival of large numbers of settlers to the area shapes the most public and current political debate about the area. Largely unoccupied up to 1990, settlers came to Old Fadama in various waves through the 1990s. A number of urban emergencies facilitated population growth. First, the AMA embarked on decongestion exercises in 1991 and 2005 to "temporarily" remove hawkers from major intersections around Accra. The 1991 exercise relocated hawkers to the edge of Agbogbloshie on the Abossey Okai main road. Second, in a separate exercise in 1993, AMA relocated the yam market to Old Fadama (COHRE 2004). Yams involve extensive labor: from traders to truckers to security personnel who are essential to guard the produce because of poor storage facilities. According to COHRE (2004, 19) "these criteria created an initial demand for trustworthy labor, which was achieved by bringing people in from the food producing areas." In turn, trucks needed repairs from time to time so requisite services also developed (welders, mechanical, tire, repair shops, etc.). As the market became established, workers came and stayed; the market served home and workplace functions (COHRE 2004, 19). Over time, the need for additional accommodations arose and temporary ones were built. The consolidation of the yam market in turn led to the emergence of a larger wholesale food market. Third, a series of land struggles in northern Ghana in 1995 involving the Kokomba, Nanumba and Dadomab peoples displaced thousands, and many made their way to urban Accra. Fourth, the population of the entire area continues to grow as migrants within Accra, across Ghana, and from proximate states (e.g., Niger, Nigeria, Liberia, Sierra Leone) find it unaffordable to rent accommodations in established residential areas. The Old Fadama area offers migrants the cheapest rents in the city as well as a proximate location to the central markets in the city, where many migrants seek casual and informal employment. The settlers have been careful to respect particular Ga shrines and to stabilize the political environment with the local stool as much as possible. Older settlers claim to have respected the Ga landowner by their payments of rents for a number of years.[11]

Since 2001, the debate around "Agbogbloshie/Old Fadama," "Old Fadama," and/or "Sodom and Gomorrah" has reached a fever pitch. The media designation "Sodom and Gomorrah" draws on the dramatic biblical story in the book of Genesis of settlement destruction by fire and brimstone. This representation has been employed by settlement detractors (including the Accra municipal authority until recently and the main national newspaper) calling for demolition of the settlement as well as removal of all of "the invaders" from the land (*Daily Graphic* 2002a, 17). The media describe the settlement as "out of place," "a no-man's land" as well as "a hideout for armed robbers, prostitutes, drug pushers and all kinds of squatters" (*News from Africa* 2002, 1). The government advocated a politics of nonrecognition toward the settlers, arguing the settlement's existence undermines an adjacent environmental restoration project, noting that "its location vis-à-vis the CBD is an eye sore as well as a major source of pollution" (AMA and Ministry of Works and Housing 2002, 3).

The area achieved notoriety on July 31, 1993 when 400 houses were affected by a dawn sweep that evicted people from public land (Accra Studio 2003, 132). Subsequently, on May 28, 2002, the AMA served an eviction notice on the entire population of Old Fadama. Community residents responded with an appeal to the High Court for an injunction to restrain the local municipality from following through. The Accra High Court rejected the community's request, and on July 24, 2002, upheld the evictions. During the summer 2002 community leaders requested international help, and efforts at grassroots globalization commenced. Efforts at grassroots globalization connect particular Accra citizens at a variety of scales and create political linkages that crisscross the globe.

11. Interview Samuel Tetteh, chair of the Ashiedu Keteke Sub-Metro, May 9, 2005.

Current politics centers on the delineation and the geographical relationship between the settlements and the lagoon and on who has the legal rights to the area. The debate raises issues about the legality of settlements, whether the settlers are original residents or invaders, whether occupation undermines the government's environmental and urban planning objectives, and whether the government is not complying with the original executive instrument. Various claims and counterclaims are being made in the legal and policy environments.

## LAND CLAIMS: THE GLOBALIZING PARADOX

The globalizing paradox centers on the issue of whether a traditional land system can meet the more extensive demands on accommodation and space in an economy that is driven more by global fluxes. Increasingly, what passes for tradition in land matters is often little more than a caricature of what existed quite some time ago. Significant portions of traditional lands in Accra have been commodified (albeit to varying degrees in different places), and the trend seems likely to continue. One of the striking features of the globalizing city is that many squatters in Accra are landed individuals from some other locale. A dilemma is whether universal rights to housing can be accommodated within the confines of the current Accra land environment, incorporating mixes of market principles and traditional land system principles. Many urbanites find themselves outside of the two systems. As a result, former cultural breaks on individuals' illegal occupation of land have been erased by the immediate shelter crisis.

Most city residents have opinions on what should happen to the settlers and the area. A number of high-profile groups (e.g., the donor community and the Ga Traditional Council) with considerable political clout have taken public positions of silence. Instead, both parties exercise power by influencing the government behind the scenes. Therefore, the debate is now centered on three main stakeholders: the government and local authorities; the settlers and their support organizations (CEPIL, PD, and GHPF); and the GaDangme, a local political organization. The GaDangme are vocal and provocative, arguing that neither the squatters nor the government has any rights to Ga lands in Accra.

The debate can be divided into two phases. The first phase concentrated on legal aspects. The major stakeholders followed their respective legal positions and policy stances. Phase two is focused on dialogue between the government, the settlers and NGOs, and international connections are helping to mediate as well as facilitate discussion. Ironically, community control of Old Fadama/Abogbloshie now requires alliances between seemingly disconnected scales, creating a new benchmark in an important land question.

## Government and its Institutions

*Negotiation position*: The government position represents a large array of institutions with particular policy domains. There is general agreement among the institutions that Old Fadama is a settlement created by the occupation of land without the permission of the landowner (in this case the government). It is mainly populated by displaced persons from northern Ghana. Legally, the government believes the settlers should be removed before twelve years of occupation (the twelve-year limitation decree), when under Ghanaian law, settlers could claim prescriptive title and rights to compensation. The government makes an important legal distinction between the two settlements: Agbogbloshie residents are informal settlers but not squatters, whereas Old Fadama settlers are considered squatters and thus should be evicted. The government relies on legal, land, and housing experts as well as on land and planning laws to bolster its position.

*Policy implications*: The government has no housing or shelter policy for the urban poor so its stance reflects the central position of a number of established policy domains. Continued occupation threatens the restoration of Accra's most important marine resource and undermines urban planning efforts around the CBD. For instance, the government's current Strategic Planning map designates the entire area as a green space for future recreational use. Moreover, continued illegal occupation, and particularly the scale of the occupation, also sets a bad precedent for urban land policies. Government officials emphasize the additional costs in the form of extra interest payments that are being incurred by the government because of delays in completion of the project.[12] With regards to international policy environment, the government emphasizes that KLERP loan terms require the removal of settlers to assist in the completion of the restoration project (UN-Habitat 2005, 85).[13] Privately, government officials emphasize that the government's international image is at stake and that this is important for a country that markets itself as a West African showcase of democracy.

*GaDangme*

*Negotiation position*: GaDangme is a political organization established in 1999.[14] Its membership is open to all members of the GaDangme traditional ethnic grouping. The organization emerged to counter the situation where "the GaDangme are falling behind as Ghana moves forward" (GaDangme Council 2002, 16). Specifically, the GaDangme Council (2002, 16) claims "their identity is increasingly being submerged and that their customs and traditions have been disregarded or treated with contempt by foreigners" (e.g., ban on drumming and noise making during Accra's annual Ga "Hommowo" festival). The organization's position is propagated by newspaper advertisements, public lectures, marches, popular writings, and other avenues. The GaDangme organization views the land questions through a local political prism with strong associations between land and ethnicity. Its position on Old Fadama/Agbogbloshie centers on four claims. The first is the government has ignored encroachments in the area. They also claim it has not acted appropriately in using GaDangme land in the public's interest. For instance, the organization claims that governmental plans to abandon the Accra railway station and current misallocation of land for industrial use

12. Interview with Sub-Metro director, May 12, 2005.

13. Newspapers sources put the loan penalties at US$30,000 per month (Gri Newsreel 2003).

14. It registered as an official NGO in June 2000, claiming that it is a nonpolitical, nonpartisan, nonreligious and nonprofit group (GaDangme Council 2002, 17). Its political agenda is well outlined in its publications, and it has become much more of a political organization since its establishment.

instead of environmental restoration require the government to return the land to the allodial owners, in this case particular Ga families. In addition, because Ga land is being occupied by squatters, the third claim is trespassers have no rights to compensation nor should they be given a resettlement option. Finally, the settlement of non-Gas on Ga lands needs to be opposed because it has the potential to change the demographic balance of the city. Two Ga families are undertaking legal proceedings against the government. Both are arguing in litigation that they are the rightful owners with legal documents and are seeking compensation.[15]

*Policy implications*: The strategy is to influence the development of a new national land policy that will be more sensitive to origins of land ownership patterns (particularly with reference to original Ga lands in Accra). In the interim, the organization demands governmental compensation for members' large losses of lands to national development purposes (Gymiah-Boadi and Asante 2003; GaDangme Council 1999). GaDangme Youth, a vocal sectional group of the organization, has held demonstrations and marches to voice its concerns. During these demonstration members mounted placards that read "give us our land back," "beware of potential bloodshed," and "Ga land keep off" (*Ghana Chronicle* 2001, 2).

## The Settlers and the NGOs

*Negotiation position*: The area has been recently settled by economic migrants, many of whom participate in the informal economy of Accra, particularly the food sector. Contemporary Agbogbloshie/Old Fadama is simply "a microcosm of a city where most live and work informally" (COHRE 2004, 4). There are some original settlers in the area who were not adequately

---

15. Interview with Bright O. Akwetey (Akwetey & Associates), who represents both families, May 10, 2005. Two families claim 80 percent of the entire area of Old Fadama/ Agbogbloshie. The J. E. Mettle family claims an area roughly corresponding to Agbogbloshie as its land, and the case is in the local court. The Ablorh Mills family is preparing to go to court claiming an area largely corresponding to Old Fatima. Both families claim that they have the legal document signed by King Tackie of Accra in 1896 gifting them the land with an accompanying site plan demarcating the boundaries.

compensated by the government when it acquired their land. Many would consider resettlement if they were invited to participate in relocation decision making and/or adequately compensated.

*Policy implications*: Their position exposes the government's failure to address the housing situation of the poor. The groups argue that people squat because there are no alternatives considering the land and housing market. They seek to give poverty a human face and to emphasize their contribution to the urban economy built around their provision of food. A proper, upgraded settlement can coexist with lagoon environmental restoration. Development is not just about showpiece projects like KLERP but also about integrating social, economic, and environmental goals (COHRE 2004). Emphasizing housing and shelter as opposed to land, the settlers want to stay clear from land politics, particularly a land politics of ethnicity.

## GLOBALIZING FROM BELOW: THE SETTLERS AND NGO PARTNERSHIPS

### *Political Horizons Prior to Globalizing Transformation*

Old Fadama and Agbogbloshie settlements had robust social and political orders since the early stage of their formation (as opposed to alternative representations of chaos). But their community frameworks were not legible to the formal policy community, which was in denial about landlessness/homelessness and the living conditions of the poor. That representatives of the Old Fadama community approached CEPIL and started legal proceedings against the AMA is a good illustration of the informal world being organized enough to act in the legal formal world. Up to 2002, the settlers combined local legal action and local political pressure through the main political parties to halt the eviction. The settlers' modus operandi was survival. Before 2002, political order inside the communities was maintained by group and overlapping hierarchies.

A thumbnail sketch of the main groups and their coexistence before their current political transformation is important to present. Various northern factions had a number of traditional chiefs who were leaders to community constituents. These northern groups also had national political party allegiances, and religious leaders held considerable power within their congregations. Slumlords and local mafia wielded much influence, and exercised power and instigated community action in particular instances, such as opposition to army and police coordinated criminal searches inside the area. Another powerful and often floating group (crossing political, ethnic, and religious lines) within the communities are "the opinion leaders." Typically drawn from the youth and working behind the scenes, they held considerable power in terms of representing the community, particularly in dealing with outside organizations. "Opinion leaders" were pivotal in strategizing about evictions and were less affected by the village pressures that could be exerted on traditional and religious leaders from their former communities of origin.

Just like all communities, political struggles existed within and among these groups, but detailing these goes beyond the scope of this research. Most important to my research is that these groups formed a common political front to oppose the threat of evictions, and that front involved mobilizing constituents to register to vote, to sign petitions, etc. Through their political party affiliations (both the New Patriotic Party and the National Democratic Congress have branch office in Old Fadama), the groups made it known that there were 20,000 registered voters in the settlements. The community groups were able to hold a united front until the July 24, 2002 Accra High Court ruling that the occupation was illegal. An appeal was considered in August 2002 but was not followed through by community representatives (UN-Habitat 2005). In the meantime, the government delayed the evictions, stalling on the implementation of an unpopular and a logistically difficult decision (UN-Habitat 2005). Instead, the government explored alternatives (at least on the surface), such as the possibility of settler relocation to another (yet unnamed) location.[16] The communities' resistance politics began to come apart at the seams. Postlitigation fatigue set in among the main activists around the time that tribal politics among northern groups

16. During the legal proceedings, a rural market location (Kasao on Cape Coast Road) was mentioned as a possible location for resettlement, but the settlers made it clear they would only consider an Accra location. AMA officials confirm that no formal resettlement plan has been drawn up as of May 2005.

were escalating. The beheading of a northern Dagbon chief in March 2002 (along with forty Yendi townspeople) spilled over into the local community (*Daily Graphic* 2002b). The northern groups became more and more factionalized, and coordinating activities on behalf of the entire communities became impossible.

*Globalizing from Below: Geographies that Connect
Accra-Cape Town, and Beyond*

In August 2000, community settlers sought legal support from the Centre for Public Interest Law (CEPIL). CEPIL is a rights-based, nongovernmental legal advocacy group that seeks justice for the poor. The seeds of connecting the community to international organizations started with CEPIL contacting the Centre on Housing Rights and Evictions (COHRE) to request legal support. COHRE, headquartered in Geneva, is the leading international human rights organization that campaigns for the protection of housing rights and against forced evictions. COHRE's involvement in the legal proceeding enabled the community to jump scales and act in concert with an international organization, and to begin to imagine other possibilities. The court's final decision was interpreted as a legal victory for government but a political victory for the community. International pressure was then placed on the government not to evict the settlers without considering alternatives or without consulting the community. Through COHRE's involvement and briefings, SDI officials became involved in the situation. Coinciding with SDI attending an international conference in Ghana, SDI officials visited the settlement. Subsequently, SDI became involved and attempted to develop a new kind of community solidarity; one that linked the urban poor across national, ethnic, religious, and international lines. The SDI model was started in Old Fadama in November 2003, and this became the learning experience to be replicated in Agbogbloshie in May 2004 and then in other communities across Ghana. It commenced in Old Fadama when Rose Molokoane, SDI board member and informal settler from Western Pretoria, led a "town hall" meeting in the heart of the factionalized slum. SDI appeared to offer a cosmopolitan perspective promoting a sense of global citizenship rather than being confined to local, regional, and national spaces. The SDI methodology involves various instruments, such as daily savings, the collection of these monies, horizontal exchanges, vertical exchanges, local projects (drainage, demolition after fires, road clearing), and self-enumerations, working with NGOs to establish dialogue with formal institutions (Mitlin and Satterthwaite 2004). Above all else, these actions linked the settlers with a SDI head office in Cape Town (subsequently they were facilitated by a local NGO: PD).[17] SDI facilitated settlers' connections with squatters and slum dwellers internationally; fostering their participation in a movement among the urban poor of developing countries.

Important in this particular instance, the Old Fadama federation began to speak for as well as organize the community. The leadership was derived from various existing political groupings in the community and from involved members who had not been active politically before (including many women). Opinion leaders supported these efforts, and strong support emerged for a global strategy to deal with the local situation. In June 2005, Old Fadama/Agbogbloshie federations had registered 3,500 members. It is important to acknowledge that the settlers' incorporation of SDI methodology into practice meant their efforts have sought to transform (rather than overturn or replace) local political institutions (particularly state and municipal authorities) and to make it more inclusive of the poor and more responsive to squatter citizens.

The community has already registered a number of political achievements:

1. *The cessation of evictions and acknowledgment of the phenomenon of urban marginalization: vital first steps in the policy process.* By their actions, members have challenged many of the stereotypes of squatters, including the naming of the area and the marginalization of squatters in various political arenas. Even though the community still remains under threat, the organizers have been able to buy time with the city. Through their networking, they have been able to turn the tables around on the government and take the initiative, demonstrating that the city has no policy to deal with the urban poor. Moreover, the settlers have questioned governmental definitions of poverty and homelessness, and forced the government to acknowledge the

---

17. PD registered as an NGO in December 2003 to build and support an urban federation of the poor in Ghana. PD is affiliated with SDI.

extent and scale of poverty. By bringing attention to the matter, the UNDP implemented a new reporting requirement mandating Ghana's Ministry of Works and Housing to incorporate a slum inventory into its annual reports.

2. *The development of citywide and national solidarity.* The community has participated in community exchanges with other groups in the Greater Accra region (Ashaiman, Avenore, etc.). While exchanges serve many needs, the most important is for the poor to reach out, connect, and create strong personal bonds with members of other communities that are in similar situations. Interaction of Old Fatima's residents with communities in six of the ten national regions is evidence of a new political movement based on a federation among the poor. The process of federating illustrates that "community" in this context does not have to be based just on locality; it is geographically far more extensive, drawing on squatter communities around the world. By federating, the poor organize and command a voice in both local and global policies that pertain to housing the poor.

3. *Local-global connections.* Old Fadama community leaders participate in horizontal exchange as cross-cultural exercises. For example, two community leaders from Old Fadama visited South Africa in the first exchange between the emerging Ghanaian federation and an established federation. Representatives had the opportunity to deepen their knowledge about community-led development and to learn about the importance of local-to-global connections in supporting slum upgrading. Five additional international exchanges (Thailand, Kenya, Nepal, Cambodia, India) have taken place in 2004 and 2005. Certainly, the SDI head office in Cape Town is a major hub in shaping the formation of these connections. All of these exchanges have involved at least one community leader from the Old Fatima/Agbogbloshie settlement. Leaders involved in the exchange report at as many Federation weekly meetings as possible when they return. One community leader said, "we now have traveled more and acquired more knowledge than the AMA leaders that seek to evict us."[18]

Certainly working with PD and SDI has dramatically increased the exposure of community leadership to international organizations, the international press, academics, and NGOs. The settlers, with the help of their

18. Group interview, May 7, 2005, with Tunetya, the first savings group in Accra.

NGO partners, were even successful in filming a short documentary about the settlement from the settlers' perspective at the World Urban Forum in Barcelona in September 2004. Taking this initiative surprised municipal authorities who responded by holding discussions with the settlers and NGOs to resolve the deadlock (UN-Habitat 2005, 85). Almost weekly now, the Old Fatima community receives a visit from some type of international delegation, and typically this involves their participation in the process of documenting their place in the city. Community leaders express that their strategy at present involves an explicit global dimension. As they put it, "the AMA is only one small player in a bigger world."[19] There is a realization that international pressure can be a very powerful force in strategizing about their situation. Moreover, this realization includes a keen awareness that they can draw on international expertise and straddle the worlds of global, national, and local policies; utilize conceptualizations from the formal housing policy worlds and present solid data—city and country wide as well as cross-national analysis—including alternatives.

4. *The development of new relationships with local authorities and the government.* By organizing at the grassroots, the settlers enjoy a greater degree of legitimacy in the eyes of policy makers and multilateral organizations. Throughout 2004 and 2005, government's strategy has shifted from an uncompromising eviction position to one that currently involves dialogue among NGOs, NGOs, residents groups, and local authorities. Four important developments have taken place that may influence the formulation of a more comprehensive housing policy for the urban poor.

First, members of the first savings group in Old Fatima and SDI representatives held a meeting with the Sub-Metro director to explain the SDI model and to put local developments into a global context.[20] Second, the settlers have participated in two roundtable discussions with NGOs, government institutions, real estate developers, and the press.[21] Building on

19. Interview with Tunetya savings group, May 7, 2005.

20. The meeting took place on February 23, 2004. The SDI Web site details this meeting; see http://www.sdinet.org/reports/r28.htm.

21. The first roundtable was organized by CHF International (an NGO concerned with housing and micro-finance in developing countries) and was held in April 2005. It was

their partnerships and alliances with other epistemological communities, the settlers have been able to legitimize their role in the urban policy process as well as find their place in local urban politics. Third, in February 2005 government welcomed a UN-Habitat mission to investigate the Old Fadama/Agbogbloshie settlement, and it commenced a dialogue with the UN mission on the situation (UN-Habitat 2005, annex 6). Subsequently, UN-Habitat established an office in August 2005 with a mandate to provide technical and logistical support to slum upgrading in Accra. Fourth, the minister of Tourism and Modernization of the capital city on November 14, 2005 formally requested the support of PD in conducting an enumeration of the settlement. By so doing, the government is taking an important step in urban poor housing policy action. However, internal community obstacles have prevented the enumeration from being completed. During a scheduled enumeration exercise in April 2006 one enumerator was assaulted and taken to the hospital. Subsequently, the enumeration was put on hold and negotiations among the stakeholders have taken place since to resolve tensions over how to obtain greater community participation.

## CONCLUSIONS

The emergence and consolidation of the human settlements at Old Fadama and Agbogbloshie represents a new land phenomenon in Accra. Their formation challenges the traditional view among policy makers and academics that squatter settlements are absent from West African cities. The evolution of the settlements at Old Fatima and Agbogbloshie shows that when large parcels of land in a government acquisition of lands remain idle, land occupation is a reality. In this particular instance, the local municipality's stopgap policies

---

significant because PD introduced the urban poor to speak from themselves on urban poverty and the housing crisis. Several members from Old Fatima spoke about their present conditions and put forward solutions. The second roundtable, "National 2015 Housing Strategy: Policy Review and Action Planning: Strategizing Towards the Millennium Development Goals," was organized by the Ministry of Works and Housing, and took place on May 25 and 26, 2005. Architects, ministry officials, UN-Habitat, the Building and Road Research Institute, PD, and the informal settlers participated.

and temporary measures (the removal of hawkers and relocation of markets) had significant ramifications because they occurred during a time when the government had no policy to deal with urban poor. Moreover, the urban poor faced an emergency because of their inability to afford land and rents.

There is evidence of a globalizing from below among members of the urban poor in Accra. My case study shows that the urban poor and their support organizations are going forth into the world and consequently repositioning themselves within the local urban political context. In this new political landscape, locally rooted but globally connected groups have emerged to address issues of homelessness, housing for the poor, and landlessness. From their point of view, the ability of their locality to continue to exist depends now more on its position within a larger global world. The poor have also been strengthened in their efforts to bring issues onto the global state by COHRE's decision to move its African regional headquarters to Accra.

The settlers are using a NGO-initiated support-based approach. Previous efforts at slum upgrading in Ghana were either externally designed by the World Bank (e.g., Urban 4) or government-initiated support-based interventions. The NGO-initiated effort represents a very different approach to the emerging commodification and individualization of land in private middle and upper-income housing. It is also very different from the conventional traditional land and home ownership that prevails on traditional lands. Because of the efforts at globalization from below, the government and UN-Habitat are talking about supporting a NGO-initiated interventionist approach. The scholarly literature on appropriate informal settlement intervention in South Africa, Brazil, India, and Zambia should provide some important lessons on how best to proceed (Huchzermeyer 2001; Huchzermeyer 2004).

It is too early to assess the success or failure of Old Fadama/Agbogbloshie grassroots political activities. Many questions remain unanswered at this stage, such as whether the settlers will be allowed to stay or relocated and under what conditions. It seems highly unlikely that government bulldozers would be able to reign "fire and brimstone" on the settlers. How the settlers and their NGO partners will deal with the geographical tension inherent in prosecuting multiscalar politics and balance local struggles and international networks is far from clear (Routledge 2003).

We also do not know if the settlers will want to continue to participate actively in SDI activities if their tangible goal of obtaining housing is achieved. As Robins has emphasized (2004, 27) "social capital, like global capital, can be very fluid—and fickle; here today, gone tomorrow." However, its "spatial fix" at particular moments in the evolution of urbanization (in places like Old Fatima) can make a major change in the way the urban land use policies and transformations are reconsidered and possibly remade. The capacity of scaling-up development may dwindle after other stakeholders reposition themselves to respond to the new realities on the ground. Nevertheless, the current dialogue between NGOs, NGOS, academics, activists and policy makers in different societies as well as different places are allowing for the democratization of certain aspects of globalization knowledge and practice (Robins 2004). These collaborations may not resolve the great unevenness in economic and political power, but they are allowing Accra squatters to take their issues "out of place."

# 7

# Conclusions

THERE ARE THREE TRENDS that are troubling with regards to the two most salient conceptualizations of urban economies in Africa. First, there is an unequal geography to urban theory, urban scholarship and urban research, as well as a bias toward examining urban planning centered on the histories and experiences of world-cities (Harrison 2006; Robinson 2006). The theory, data, and reasoning are not always helpful for assessing urban development in globalizing cities. Indeed, it even may be unhelpful (Robinson 2006). My research has sought to explore the kinds of data and to identify the most important processes and spatial outcomes that are at the center of the transformation of globalizing cities. Because world-city scholarship cannot be directly applied, a more sensible research approach is to build an understanding of globalizing cities from the ground upward. Looking out from Accra as a prism sheds important light on its globalizing experiences, and understanding its emerging space economy may provide an important guide for studying globalizing cities in general. However, I am mindful not to present Accra as a paradigmatic city. There is a great diversity of cities in Africa and not all of them are globalizing. Some cities still remain peripheral to globalization processes, particularly cities within conflict regions (e.g., Kinshasa) and cities that lie in states that have weak records of implementing liberalization policies (e.g., Maputo). However, even in this case, South African companies establishing large retail operations in Maputo have drawn even Mozambique into the global economy (Miller 2007). Studying the configurations of these globalizing relations and putting African cities at the center of the analysis is much more important than making facile comparisons with world-cities.

Second, if world-city researchers are guilty of overlooking the internationalization of cities in Africa, so too are domestic urban policy makers within African states. It is ironic that analyses before the 1980s emphasized the impact of external forces on urban development, but in the liberalization era, government policy makers have tended to concentrate almost exclusively on internal determinants of urban and national economies once market-orientated policies are introduced. Policy makers' over emphasis on letting the market work has indirectly focused exclusive attention on domestic economic policies, governance, national land policy, and rent-seeking behavior. As a result, within African states, theories that frame urban economies within the context of external forces have been discredited and/or placed on the defensive. Emphasis on internal affairs serves as a useful corrective to the previous excessive focus on the external determinants of colonial economies. However, the domestic lens fails to capture the dynamic and synergistic effects of international sources of urban change.

Too often, cities in Africa have been viewed as marginal to global economic processes, characterized by "black holes and loose connections" (Short 2004a, 295). Media sources have provided even more damning critiques of African governments' failures in globalization efforts. For example, the *Economist* (2001, 12), commenting on the widening per capita income gaps between the United States and Africa, states that it would "be wrong to blame globalization for holding Africa back. Africa has been left out of the global economy, partly because governments used to prefer it that way." Typically, African governments counter that their economic fragility is based on not being globalized enough. Both of these viewpoints miss a proper understanding of globalizing cities. It is very apparent that national statistics fail to account for what is unfolding in globalizing cities. Significant changes in trade, Gross National Product Per Capita (GNPPC), and national economic growth rates have not been registered. Instead, government policy makers have put many urban economies on a low economic growth trajectory, incorporating highly uneven rates of economic development and underdevelopment, which condition the levels and types of integration that take place within the global economy. The promise of globalization was supposed to result in observable achievements in specific macroeconomic indicators. It has not. Because globalization is not visible in changes in key macroeconomic indicators does not mean it is not present! Nor does it mean that domestic factors can adequately explain the newer trends on the ground.

Third, connections in globalizing cities are glued together differently, and this aspect of urban economies needs more emphasis. Connections are formed and cemented in domestic environments where most laws have not been updated since the colonial period. However, the reach of the international environment is much more extensive and the nexus between the international and domestic environments has been much more of a gray area characterized by intermingling. Globalizing city environments exhibit weaknesses in market, legal, financial, and technology systems. Informality rather than formal legal contracts and small investments rather than large capital investments are the norm. Financial and real estate systems provide good examples. In the financial arena, the formal systems cater mainly for large scale investors, forcing the majority to finance residential investments out of personal savings and loans from the informal sector. The formal real estate environment caters mainly to expatriates, forcing the majority to build incrementally and informally. As a result, the business and real estate environments are disorganized and fragmented. However, within these environments there are tightly knit, distinct segments that are tied together in very limited ways. Segments of the imperfect market are very tight, involve small sums of capital and few players, but exhibit a robustness that allows them to operate within globalizing city and sometimes even to reach across borders. Because many agents in the globalizing city are able to jump scales and deploy foreign capital and/or expertise further undermines the weak and outdated frameworks that prevail in the urban environment.

## UNFOLDING GLOBALIZATION IN ACCRA

At first glance, Accra seems far removed from globalization processes. On closer inspection, Accra shows all kinds of evidence of an increasing importance of the international dimension of urban change. The Accra data show the following:

• The government is continuing to pursue the foreign sector to participate in urban development through policies that promote and sustain a climate that encourages foreign participation.

• Over 2,000 foreign companies have been established since the mid-1980s.

- New housing is mostly paid for out of savings. Average new house constructions are way out of sync with local salaries, pointing to alternative and oftentimes foreign sources of income.
- Remittance flows now account for a significant portion of the national economy.
- Some US$2 billion worth of residential properties are entering the property market, of sorts.
- Returnee migrants are coming back home in significant numbers, and their investments are having an impact on local economic development.
- Nonresident Ghanaians are active in buying property, sending money back home, sustaining families, helping fuel explosive growth in the housing sector, and contributing funds for all sorts of bootstrap enterprises with local partners.
- Wealthier family members paying for the costs of housing for poorer family members is resulting in making parts of neighborhoods economically diverse.
- Housing preferences are shifted toward villa-style dwellings and private enclaves (when they can be afforded) and away from compound housing.
- Slum dwellers are participating in international exchanges and forging international relationships.

The idealism of the liberalization era in Ghana has enabled global policy designs to meet local histories and realities. Liberalization policies have not resulted in diversifying the economic base; vibrant EPZs and large manufacturing industrial clusters have not been created, and global outsourcing has only a modest presence. Instead, free market-oriented policies have resulted in unintended outcomes in investments, residential building, migrations, unplanned spatial development, and large-scale remittances. We can be sure that these changes are fueling further transformations in the globalizing process. Ironically, liberalization policies designed to integrate Accra into the global economy failed to predict the outcomes because there was little or no policy consideration given to the strategic form of integration required to best serve Ghana's development needs. Instead, liberalization policies resulted in increasing gaps in income, shelter, and employment opportunities. Davis (2006, 6) is stretching the truth by characterizing the Accra corridor "stretching from Accra to Benin City as the biggest single footprint of poverty on earth." However, globalizing spaces are only denting the larger economically marginalized landscape. Allowing market forces to operate before various institutional environments (land, legal, financial, business, and educational) could be restructured in a purposeful way, unintentionally resulting in economic development à la carte from transnationals and select groups of urbanities. It also has exacerbated poverty in the city.

Colliding modernities are shaping globalizing processes. First, in the land arena, foreign capital intersects with traditional land arrangements. Access to urban land operates both within elements of a free market and in the context of a legal traditional land system. In some urban land acquisitions there has been a formalization of informalization—paying market values and registering parcels of land that exist under the national traditional land-law system. At the same time, there has been an infomalization of the formal land market, where some individuals representing landed families, stools, and other vested parties have unaccounted profits from the sale of traditional land.

Second, in the land and real estate market there is considerable confusion among the government, traditional leaders, market dealers, and the public about whose information is reliable, credible, and legitimate (Jones 2003). The problems stem from two categories of land information (Hammond 2006, 396). Category one information is the "direct transaction information produced from the original acquisition or from the exchange of property rights" (Hammond 2006, 396) and is generally only known to the specific transacting parties. Category two information is the "officially processed, compressed and simplified version of category one information" (Hammond, 2006, 396). Officially, in Ghana only category two information is considered legitimate. However, because the vast majority of transactions do not get recorded into category two information (the conversion process takes up to 600 days), there are huge information gaps and secrets about land in Accra and traditional land information does not correspond to government and/or market dealer information.

The residential buildings that have been erected on traditional lands are typically modern bungalows/villas and sometimes apartments; only rarely are traditional compound dwelling units built. Compound housing has many advantages including lower costs to build, suiting traditional inheritance patterns, and allowing the sharing of services within the context of multi-habitation (Andersen et al. 2006). Studies suggest that western-style nuclear family household is seen by most people as a "modern ideal" and that compound house is viewed as a "symbol of the past" (Andersen et al. 2006, 13). The demise of compound houses is leaving a gaping hole in the housing supply of low-income households, a demographic groups that represents that majority of the urban population (Andersen et al. 2006). Moreover, the transformation in land ownership is also coupled with a change in architectural styles and tastes. Western-style dwelling spaces and arrangements are being cut from the urban experience of global cities and pasted onto a traditional society and land system. However, these trends raise the housing policy issue of what has been lost in the changing preferences and what is being achieved by the widespread villa development and spread of private gated communities that now characterize a significant portion of the residential building sector.

Second, the informal sector provides most credit. Less than 5 percent of Ghanaians have bank accounts, and access to formal credit is also very limited (*Ghanaian Chronicle* 2004, 1). Individuals rely on remittances, local family and friends, and/or loan sharks. Access to capital is the major barrier to home and business ownership. My household surveys revealed that 60 percent of individuals' money supply is outside of formal financial institutions like banks. Higher entry costs have put the breaks on Accra households dividing up family incomes, spreading it around to the extended family, and engaging in traditional financial thinking: what Bowditch (1999, 50) has termed "chop economics." Instead, many urban residents are emphasizing economic rationality in searching for plots, buildings, and business opportunities to accumulate capital. Buying residential properties and starting small businesses have become the most widespread savings program in Accra. However, few properties and businesses are ever sold so it is unknown how liquid these investments will be in the long-term. Since 2004, micro-credit agencies have had a bigger presence in Accra and have offered alternative access of credit. For instance, the Chicago-based Opportunity International loaned US$6.2 million during its first two years of operation in Accra (Agyepong 2006). It aims to serve 50,000 clients in Ghana by the end of 2006 (Agyepong 2006, 1). However, in many ways international micro-credit agencies represent yet another development in the trend of grassroots capitalism through a foreign source.

Third, a functioning market requires access of information and relevant data to make informed decisions about the market. There are serious information shortcomings (e.g., about land and business ownership, property transactions, profits and losses from investments, tax records, and reliable maps of land ownership) in Ghana. Sparse data allow globalizing processes to unfold in silence and in secret. Furthermore, the lack of transparency in the land and business environments removes government further from the market, except in instances where government officials use their power and position to assume gatekeeper and/or broker roles. Government officials on private cell phones is a regular sight at the Lands Commission, where answers to data requests from property developers, chiefs, interested buyers, and foreigners are provided; information can be provided that is never officially published nor archived in a way that ensures equal and fair access. The inability to combine traditional and modern property registration systems is a good example of the way both land systems fail. It also explains why so many property transactions reside in between and how both traditional and modern gatekeepers have been empowered at the expense of creating a fairer market. Data shortcomings help cement ties between some traditional leaders and investment capitalists, producing unlikely alliances. It encourages opportunistic behaviors. Traditional societies have always privileged the wealthy, the well-connected, and the gatekeepers of knowledge. Globalizing Accra privileges a different type of expertise that draws on and combines global as well as local knowledge. As Hammond (2006, 395) emphasizes "the privileged few are able to obtain opportunistic positions that influence the outcome of (real estate) market transactions enormously." Combining both worlds, individuals have been able to find plots, build, and pay for new houses, and establish new businesses. Navigating this imperfect market requires specialized knowledge, domestic and foreign networks, and foreign cash, considering the moderate local salaries and the inflationary environment. The lack of data on the property market as well as the dearth of information means buyers and sellers act in their own way. As a result, there is a lack of proper regulation of property values: valuations are often subject to the whims of those involved in transactions (Mends 2006). This means each property is to a large extent traded on its own merit and under its own particular circumstances.

Colliding modernities result in considerable bending in socioeconomic relations. First, traditional institutions bend as traditional agents engage international capital and global trends. Traditional leaders driving luxury imported cars and engaging in property transactions with foreign investors is one extreme example of this bending. Second, foreign investors also bend. Foreign companies learn the power of "dashing" (giving local gifts and bribes) to facilitate local transactions and to ensure that their time is not tied up defending local land acquisitions. Even established companies with a global presence like the Coca-Cola Bottling Company, Ghana have had to defend their land acquisition and site for manufacturing on numerous occasions from several members of local landowning families. Several individuals representing local landowning families claim that the bottling plant is located on traditional lands and have requested to be financially compensated.[1] Foreign companies also link into the informal sector, routinely sourcing parts for machinery and equipment, subcontracting work, and hiring casual labor. Third, nonresident Ghanaians also bend in order to live global and Ghanaian lifestyles at particular times and in particular places. The transnationals who participate in the politics and economics of two countries at the same time illustrate this trend.

Fourth, wealthy Ghanaians bend by separating their financial commitments and sense of obligation to both the nuclear and extended families. Building a house for the nuclear family within a walled private gated community while also contributing to the building of a new but separate house in a different location for the extended family is a good example. Fifth, locals bend in so many ways. Most important, they have to make a living in a difficult environment to survive because the government provides little, and connected individuals deploy capital and funds from abroad in all sorts of ways. Slum dwellers might appear to be the furthest and most marginalized from the external and global world, but they too learn to bend as they act and participate in the larger world (outside of the slum and city), whereby the representatives of slum-dweller organizations work with international agencies and international media to improve their contemporary situations.

1. Interview with managing director, Ian Blackburn, July 8, 2004.

Globalization is unfolding in a widespread but unequal participation in the marketplace. Everyone is doing business in Accra irrespective of origin, age, gender, ethnicity, socioeconomic status, education, and migration experience. Most urbanites are moving money, building relationships, and searching for economic opportunities, although many engage the market through the informal sector. The liberalization environment has led to an explosion of trader entrepreneurs in the globalizing city; former small market sellers have turned into small hoteliers, importers, and real estate agents (Bowditch 1999). There are no theories that seem capable of explaining the extent to which everyone is trading and participating in the market, albeit on very unequal terms. Locals seem to be approaching the globalizing environment through a traditional market lens, drawing heavily on aspects of a community life that revolves around traditional markets (Bowditch 1999). For instance, trader-entrepreneurs are utilizing the skills and knowledge they have absorbed from their festive kin to participate in a globalizing economy. Accordingly, their networks blend business, family and neighborhoods, and their energies focus on the immediate market in familiar locations and in short-term strategies (Bowditch 1999). These locals deploy knowledge in bootstrap thinking on investment decisions. Many realize their shortcomings but proceed because they do not have an alternative and fear being left further behind in the globalizing city.

## Globalizing City: The Spatial Organization of Accra

The globalizing city exists because its circuits and circulation are fundamentally in contact with elsewhere. It no longer makes sense to conceptualize African urban environments in isolation from the rest of the world or as nonglobalized environments. My research shows that globalization processes were in the first instance ushered in from above by policies designed to attract FDI and foreign investors. Ghanaians in the diaspora also participated and benefitted from the opening up the national economy. Some members of the diaspora eventually returned to Accra; returnees are now very active in the development process, particularly in starting all sorts of bootstrap enterprises. A significant portion of returnees participate as transnational entrepreneurs, orchestrating globalization from in between. Globalization was also facilitated from below. Slum dwellers working with international NGOs like SDI to build a community among some slums dwellers and further enabled them to connect with other slum-dweller communities across Accra and internationally. International exchanges among slum-dweller communities not only served the political purpose of creating a movement of globalization from below, but in certain instances, it also led to economic exchanges. For instance, following the SDI official exchange between Accra-Nairobi in June 2004, several Old Fadama slum dwellers commenced trading textiles with their counterparts in Kibera, Nairobi.

These three movements of globalization involve the movement of capital, peoples, goods, and knowledge among global places, within the globalizing city and indirectly between the globalizing city and towns and rural localities from which city residents originate. It is the combination and the integration of formal and informal practices that is most important in globalizing cities.

Map 7.1 illustrates the five key elements in the contemporary urban-economic geography of Accra. First, there are the visible upscale residential and corporate geographies that compartmentalize the city and fragment its spatial development in fundamental ways. In the words of Graham and Marvin (2001), Accra is a good example of "splintering urbanism." The assemblage of newly built office complexes and upscale housing in low-density areas is set against decaying older residential and high-density commercial areas. There are areas that are clearly locations for the concentration of global activities. A new global CBD has emerged with a high concentration of foreign corporate firms, particularly foreign companies engaged in financial and producer services sectors. Private gated developments with expensive housing also have become concentrated in eastern Accra, in the vicinity of the airport.

Second, the inner city has remained a vibrant area, providing opportunities for trade and small enterprises. Planning efforts to relocate traders and market functions to more peripheral locations have failed. Slum clearance initiatives for the inner city have also encountered significant local opposition. Instead, new and large slums have emerged on government lands adjacent to the city center. Overall, the central city has enlarged its petty trade and food market functions in the liberalization era. To date, the inner city has not experienced urban regeneration and gentrification, common to many global cities.

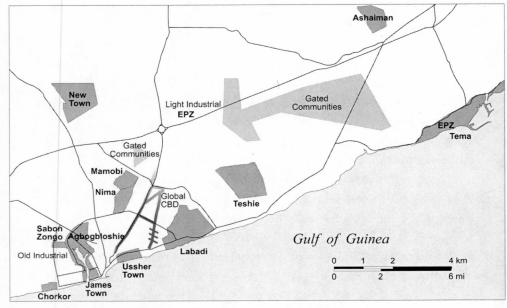

Map 7.1. Globalizing Spaces in Accra. Source: Grant 2008.

Third, slums have proliferated in many parts of the city in addition to the central city. Newer slums like Agbogbloshie/Old Fadama accommodate nearly 40,000 people in the central city, many of whom work in food trade in the central city. Slums have also appeared on the outskirts of the city; Ashaiman is the largest slum on the outskirts, and around 25,000 people live there. There are also many traditional housing areas (Jamestown, Nima, Labadi, etc.) where housing conditions have worsened, and these residential areas now must be counted as slums.

Fourth, there are specific locations in the city where the multiple interactions and overlapping realities involving both the formal economy and the informal city are concentrated. An auto repair cluster has emerged in Obessy-Okai, with a high concentration of workshops that specialize in auto parts, refurbishment and small-scale manufacturing. The inner city food markets supply restaurants and hotels throughout the city. Furniture and textile enterprises are clustered at the Trade Fair Centre in Labadi, and many enterprises source their inputs from informal sector enterprises.

Fifth, geographic clusters and concentrations of industries are evident in a number of areas. The light industrial area is an old industrial area that has expanded and contains a diversity of manufacturing enterprises specializing in brewing, printing, machinery, chemicals, and construction materials. The Spintex Industrial area houses a number companies that operate as free zone companies (e.g., Carson beauty products manufacturing) and a wide variety of construction material manufactures. The Tema Industrial area has a diversity of companies involving chemicals, food processing, textiles, and information technology.

In addition, there is an unquantifiable blending of the urban and rural dimensions of life in general across the city. The postcolonial point of view is most instructive in showing that the traditional oppositionalism of rural and urban is inaccurate in a globalizing city. Rather, these different worlds are being mapped onto one another in increasingly complex ways. Much of Accra is a "hermaphroditic landscape" (Davis 2006, 9), an environment that combines international and local living, urban and rural living, wherein a dense web of transactions ties the globalizing spaces to the world beyond Ghana as well as urban cores to the rural areas. The contrasts are striking. In Accra, informal market trade on the streets and traditional food consumption is overlaid with more modern urban living in bungalow and villa-type housing. In many individually built areas, the contemporary intermingling of urban-rural life is common. For example, people generally prepare food with traditional cooking methods, oftentimes with charcoal. Furthermore, in upscale residential areas (but not gated developments), kiosks and small enterprises are erected adjacent to residential buildings. These businesses often accommodate Ghanaian family relatives and/or festive kin, maintaining social bonds even though these relationships are on highly unequal terms. Accommodating family members in this way is the modern equivalent of village life. In many parts of the globalizing city there is no exact alternative to rural life but rather lived spaces that are neither rural nor urban, but somewhere in a process of transformation.

*Transnationalism as a Transformative Process in Globalizing Accra*

Transnationalism is a powerful source of urban transformation in a globalizing city. It may be even relatively more important in globalizing cities (compared to global/world-cities) because of the particular level of development that entails greater opportunities for smaller sums of capital that can be deployed in an emerging market environment. Because loans are so limited in Accra, transnational capital is a powerful source of change.

Transnationalism is very salient in globalizing cities. First, the transnational house is now an important feature of the residential environment. Transnational houses are found in larger numbers in many of the newly built, private, gated community developments in Accra. Gated communities play a significant role in both shaping and reflecting changing landscape meanings and values. They are paid for with imported funds (savings and earning from working abroad). Many of the houses are constructed by foreign builders with imported building materials. Transnational houses are indicative of new economic values for land, for homes, for community, and for the cementing of ties that stretch beyond Ghana's borders. Investment decisions and lifestyle values, rather than strict use-value, are important motivating factors. Owners have indicated a preference for houses in a community with other professionals and are motivated by economic prestige. Ethnicity and Ghanaian family ties seem much less important to these homeowners. Houses in gated communities are characterized by nuclear families, and owners motivated more by globalizing lifestyles than by traditional cultural considerations; although some gated community residents are still able to combine elements of both worlds.

Second, more and more individuals pursue transnational entrepreneurship. There is considerable evidence that many return migrants are engaged in transnational businesses. In many ways, these are agents in globalizing cities about which we know little. They generally fly under the radar but exhibit high participation rates in the urban economy, and they are linked to local and international business circuits; many employ their experience at home and abroad to launch bootstrap business enterprises. Generally, they start an entrepreneurial career with little prior experience and without any institutional assistance. In the process of weaving these networks, more people are entangled in transnational space, irrespective of migration history. We are a long way from the speculative claims in the theoretical literature (Brah 1996; Mohan 2006) of the native being as much a diasporian as the diasporian being a native. Nonetheless, returnees are important agents and anchors between these increasingly interrelated worlds.

Third, an increasing number of household budgets are financed from deposits from various sources that depend on activities inside as well as outside of Ghana. Remittances are an important way migrants benefit development back home. In a very quiet way, remittances are transforming the urban economy and represent a visible example of self-help. Remittances add another element to the economic diversity of the city. Their role is important in correcting household budgetary shortfalls and consumption, and for some upper-income individuals, they are a source of funding for housing or small businesses. There are many examples of these funds being used in productive ways, but there are equally as many examples of funds being flitted away. For many of the entrepreneurs interviewed, external funds were preferred to local bank loans carrying 25 to 28 percent interest rates (which many would not even quality for). For entrepreneurs in particular, remittance funds and loans from those who received remittance flows were essential to maintaining businesses, and interviewees emphasized foreign funds being typically used to expand business operations. Business owners starved of these types of investments find it hard to move beyond survivalist enterprises.

Still, there are many other urbanites who, while not transnational in the strict sense, are influenced and indirectly affected by transnationalism. In the accommodation arena (property prices and high rents) they experience the direct effects. Rising house price-to-income ratios and rental-to-income ratios illustrate this trend. There is also a larger array of spillover effects for those who have been able to raise funds abroad and to circulate these funds locally. Tensions are being expressed in local policy debates about taxing the portion of remittances that goes into housing investments (*Daily Graphic* 2006), which seems practically impossible to determine. The government would like to spend this tax money on providing housing and social amenities and on improving infrastructure. No doubt there are deep and unquantifiable psychological effects on urbanites who view an intangible and unseen external economy as equally important, if not more important, to the tangible and seen local economy in sustaining and maintaining livelihoods.

There are additional, less tangible ways that transnationalism influences society. They may encourage future migration streams, they may have an influence on eroding traditional systems, they may even play a wild card in the political process, inclining the government toward more global engagement, especially in terms of policies and laws that seek to draw even more on the diaspora.

### Mismatch Between Government Liberalization Policy Thrust and Outcomes

The rationalities of the neoliberal policy community that privilege corporate thinking were always going to encounter resistance from local communities with local traditions and local thinking. Clearly GOG has privileged corporate and market forces since 1983 in thinking big. What the global policy community and the GOG failed to anticipate was the degree to which locals could think and act globally. As a result, the globalizing city was transformed as much by ordinary individuals as by larger corporations. The business and policy elite engaged in much urban boosterism, imagining Accra as a grand "gateway city" with key hubs like the port, the airport, and the EPZ connecting the city to global commerce and anchoring Accra as a regional platform to serve West African markets. The city that is emerging is a small gateway whereby many urbanites think and act small but nonetheless use the city as a platform to connect their daily lives with the global world beyond. It is impossible to put numbers on all of these interactions, but combined they have a huge and qualitatively significant impact on the urban economy. This is such a salient feature of the Ghanaian economy that is surprising that policy makers have problems thinking about the power of the small. Accra has been constructed by one small investment decision after another rather than by some comprehensive plan targeting large-scale investors.

Clearly, it was a mammoth task to bring Ghana into the global economy through a set of liberalization policies that took place without any preparation of society and that were oblivious to the workings of the society. This shock was always going to force individuals to act in unpredictable and different ways (compared to what would be anticipated based on world-city experiences). The government spent all of its energies cultivating an investor-friendly environment. Surprisingly, little attention was given to harnessing foreign investment properly and to thinking about how investment could be used in productive ways. The impacts of globalizing processes on local capital, local employees, and especially local development were not adequately addressed. As a result, many businesses failed. Real estate deals went astray. The city grew in leaps and bounds without much spatial planning. Zoning laws were applied haphazardly and were not strictly enforced in many localities. More and more urbanites experienced further economic marginalization (Yeboah 2005). Some of the youth even went as far as taking out one-page advertisements costing US$2,000 (Yeboah 2003b) in the two leading national newspapers to change their urban landless situation in a country where, by birthright, they are supposed to be entitled to land (*Daily Graphic* 2002d). The globalizing environment means urban residents participate to various and different degrees in modernity and encounter different development experiences. Most urbanites are trapped somewhere in between globalization and underdevelopment.

The scholarly and policy communities need to turn their attention toward a better understanding of the local development impacts of globalization. Urban theory has an urgent challenge to understand the reality in which the majority of the world's population lives (mostly outside of global cities). Contemporary planning is limited by its origins within the intellectual traditions and experiences of the West (Harrison 2006). The intellectual resources needed to sustain and counterbalance this effort will have to be enormous. In the meantime, governments need to think and act more creatively.

I offer a number of practical suggestions based on my research. Focusing more on small and medium businesses as opposed to large global corporations should be an obvious place to start. Local governments must act to develop more inclusive and innovative approaches to investment so development can better serve a wider diversity of interests. For instance, policy efforts to train families and relatives of migrants on investment opportunities and business management would be a step in the right direction. Economic and urban development policies need to be better linked. Economic development has traditionally been regarded as a national responsibility, and policy toward that end has not been a traditional local authority responsibility, so municipalities have neither the legislative base nor the policy expertise to tackle it. Governance failures, infrastructure deficiencies, and spatial planning failures have meant urban environments are not conducive to either efficient or transparent economic operation (Rakodi 2004). Remedying this major policy oversight requires better analytical and conceptual tools that acknowledge the multiple interconnections between the formal and informal sectors and modern and traditional economies. Urban and economic policy needs to be redirected toward grasping this interface. The globalizing city framework is an approach to understand the interface between globalization and traditional society, and between simultaneity and connections among different places.

## Urban Futures of Globalizing Cities

Ghana became the first country in Africa, south of the Sahara, to achieve political independence on March 6, 1957. When Ghana celebrated its fiftieth year of independence in March 2007, many questioned what has been achieved. Heated debates ensued about the development impacts of many foreign companies. Coca Cola's high-profile marketing role in the fiftieth anniversary celebrations, which included launching a commemorative coke bottle, came to symbolize the development paradox. Many asked how has it been possible for foreign companies, such as Coca-Cola, to achieve such a stranglehold on Ghanaians' wallets. Coca-Cola commenced a modest Accra bottling operation in 1956 but its country expansion has been spectacular in the last decade so that the company now sells more than two million cases per year. The Coca-Cola story just tips the surface in the way that globalization is grounded and in terms of the wider implications for budgets, diets, etc.

Besides documenting the grounding of globalization, I outlined the key features leading the transformation process in Accra and the process of becoming a globalizing city. A globalizing city may be its end state; Accra may always remain in an in-between situation so we need to develop the tools to better understand this reality.

It is important to realize, as Harrison (2006, 324) emphasizes, there is a "space of modes of place-making that go beyond the mimicry of patterns in the North." Some ways to move forward in thinking and reconceptualizing cities in the South have been put forward by postcolonial scholars. They are optimistic about a double consciousness that is emerging, "bringing together local histories into an engagement with global design that is allowing subaltern rationality to find a place alongside the formal rationalities of planning" (Harrison 2006, 326). However, as Harrison (2006, 333) points out, postcolonial thought teaches us much about the value position of other world views, but it does not inform us about the practicalities of planning and making concrete choices about specific situations. Much work also needs to be undertaken from a postcolonial perspective on how various insights can be transferred into making better policy. Harrison (2006, 331) thinks that "the most pragmatic way for policy makers and planners to proceed is to act reasonably rather than attempt the impossible task of meeting some normative criteria—where reasonableness means acting as democratically and communicatively as possible under difficult circumstances and in doing so, drawing on common sense, instinct and reasonable sentiment." Certainly this kind of thinking will get us started, but we need to go deeper. Postcolonial scholars need to be much more concrete about how empirical research should proceed and how this research should inform policymaking.

My analyses have focused on economic factors leading to urban transformation in a globalizing city. There is still much work that needs to be undertaken about the economy. We know virtually nothing about the working of slums and the kinds of enterprises and production units that are located therein, how these units contribute to the urban economy, and how they connect with the wider space economy. The economy of slums is a neglected spatiality in urban as well as economic geography. Neither Davis' (2006) conception of slums as reservoirs of surplus labor nor De Soto's (2000) conception of emerging entrepreneurs seems sufficient in fully explaining how slum economies work. There is growing evidence about certain slums being linked to the wider economy through flexible production (Davis 2006) and niche businesses being located in particular slums (COHRE 2004). Because more and more urbanites are living in slums, an understanding of the economy of slums is of major importance.

More research is necessary to understand the functioning of the land and real estate markets. Clearly, major changes are needed to reform land law, land administration, and create agreed upon public data on land and property transactions. In the meantime, there are grounds for arguing that the Accra urban residential markets need to be rethought along a variety of market dimensions (full, partial, mixed, foreign, local, insider, and outsider) and nonmarket dimensions (wholly traditional, partly traditional) in order to create more accurate typologies and assessments of residential markets.

Further research and debate are needed to clarify the social and political dynamics in a globalizing city. For instance: What are the political ramifications of a large group of urbanites becoming landless and excluded from the housing market? How will economic rationality affect traditional cultural values and attitudes of family and community? What are the tensions surrounding the role of globalizing agents in the political and cultural arenas? Significant research is needed to compare the Accra evidence to other globalizing cities and engage in debates about the comparative urban experience. Finally, at a theoretical level we need to refine and improve theorizing about globalizing cities.

The mix of informalism and formalism that is interspersed in globalizing cities may be setting a precedent for cities around the world in the twenty-first century. Furthermore, policy makers need to acknowledge and implement polices that facilitate the dynamics of the integration of the so-called formal and informal economies. It is only by properly acknowledging the ways that globalizing cities work and function that we will be able to visualize very different possibilities that may emerge, and to make concrete and precise recommendations. Only by studying the various experiences of globalizing cities rather than assessing these cities through some other normative view can we get research, scholarship, and policymaking back on the right track. The fundamental importance of developing a proper appreciation of the causes and consequences of urban processes in the globalization era cannot be overestimated—not least because the future of our world is an urban future. The globalizing city, in all likelihood, will be a permanent situation, but ever transforming. Globalizing cities are neither global nor traditional cities, neither formal nor informal cities, neither fully urban nor rural in orientation; rather they are in the process of combining. International drivers of urban development are a critical aspect in understanding globalizing cities. Globalizing cities are creating a new path in human settlement and economic development.

APPENDIX

WORKS CITED

INDEX

# APPENDIX

# Data Collection

MUCH OF THE DATA for this book are based on two survey efforts. First, a large foreign company/corporate survey conducted September to December 1999, and a related and subsequent domestic company survey in February 2000. Second, a household residential survey conducted in summer 2004. The research also draws on a number of data produced by various agencies in Ghana; for example, The Bank of Ghana, GIPC, and the GSS. In addition, I conducted numerous interviews with key agents in the urban economy such as government officials, NGO representatives, and real estate agents.

The first survey effort entailed a large foreign company survey. This survey was essential because data on foreign corporate activity in African cities are generally scarce and incomplete. Internationally monitored datasets (e.g., Dun & Bradstreet 1997; United Nations Center on Transnational Corporations 1988) provide directories on foreign companies and their affiliates abroad, but they contain information only on the largest multinational corporations in the world. In addition, these data are biased toward companies from the OECD (with the largest assets), are often out of date, and greatly underestimate the extent of foreign corporate activity in Africa.

Locally generated datasets also inadequately represent information on foreign companies. Prior to this research, there were no directories of foreign companies in Accra that were accurate or even remotely complete. Government agencies that monitor foreign investment can provide information on foreign companies, but their information relates to approved investments or collaborations, not to currently active companies. GIPC provided me with a listing of companies that had newly registered at its office. In the early days, the GIPC noted that 26 percent of all companies that have registered are not functionally operating and that some foreign companies choose not to register with the GIPC (even though they are required to by law) (Grant 2001), but GIPC data is now much more accurate. Therefore, the GIPC listing is only an estimate and cannot be taken to represent accurately the population of foreign companies in Accra.

Defining a foreign company is no easy task, but a foreign company is defined under the Ghana Investment Promotion Centre Act, 1994 (Act 478) as a company with FDI of over $10,000 for a joint-venture partnership in any sector except trading where the minimum capital requirement is US$300,000. Wholly foreign owned companies are companies with a minimum of US$50,000. The very liberal investment climate in Ghana since the early 1980s permits foreign investors to own up to 100 percent equity in companies. The data collection on foreign corporations consisted of three steps, implemented over two years: 1. the identification and mining of all available listings of foreign companies and their addresses from local sources; 2. the combination of these listings and checking for overlaps and inconsistencies to create a single master list of foreign companies and addresses; and 3. the conducting of a survey among these companies using the "total design method" (Dillman 1978). The datasets pertain to the headquarters of each company, but the "location" of a company may not be confined to the address of the headquarters. Many of the larger companies have their headquarters and managerial staff in a prime business area although administrative support work and factories are located elsewhere in the city or beyond.

I contacted all government organizations working closely with foreign companies for information. Organizations besides the GIPC that provided me with detailed information include the Divestiture Implementation Committee, the Minerals Commission, and the Ghana Free Zone Board, the Ghana Stock Exchange, and the embassies or consulates of the UK, the Netherlands, Italy, the United States, Japan, Denmark, Switzerland, Germany, France, China, and Lebanon. The lists were cross-checked for accuracy with existing business directories in Accra, including the *Ghana Telephone Directory* (1998) and the *FIT Business Directory* (1999).

The resulting master list formed the basis for the survey, which allowed a final round of corrections. Eventually, a database of 655 foreign companies was constructed. The foreign company surveys focused on company names, addresses, year of establishment, type of activity, economic sector, country of origin, company size, etc. To increase the possibility of response, the surveys were returned to a mailbox I established in Accra. The initial mail surveys were followed up by a second round of mail surveys and then by phone calls to increase response rates even further. The final response rate was around 51 percent.

A related domestic company survey was also administered. Existing data on *domestic* companies were extensive, relatively reliable, and more easily obtainable, and as a result it was not necessary to survey all of those companies. Domestic company listings used in the empirical analysis were obtained from the Ghana National

Chamber of Commerce, which produces an annual listing of domestic companies by location and type of activity. The domestic company list for Accra contained over 1,800 entries. My research efforts concentrated on surveying domestic companies in the central city. Both the foreign and domestic datasets permitted me to analyze, over time, the relative importance of foreign corporate presence in the city, the nature of foreign investment and, particularly, the geography of foreign corporate activity in comparison with domestic corporate activity.

The second survey effort collected data from household surveys designed to investigate the international dimension of the new residential land market in Accra. The absence of well-established real estate sectors means that neither government agencies nor private developers have cooperated in maintaining up-to-date data on the housing environment. Czaja and Blair's (2004) methodology for questionnaire survey research was used to design the survey. A combination of fully structured and open-ended questions was utilized in the research, and seventy questions were used in the final survey. The survey was pilot tested in May 2004 in three urban localities, and fifteen heads of households were surveyed. Subsequently, the questionnaire was revised.

The final data collection took place between June 11 and June 27, 2004. To be representative of the city, urban localities were carefully selected to reflect the east-west orientation of the city, and each of the three administrative districts were sampled. Ten residential areas were selected to provide a cross section of the types of housing areas that are incorporated into the city fabric. The sampling involved selecting among three categories: private housing areas and newly developed areas where there is a preponderance of individuals' building their own houses. East Airport, ACP estates, and Sakamono were selected as private housing areas. In addition, Trasacco Valley was later added to shed light on the gated community phenomenon. Gbawe, Ofankor, and Dansoman were chosen as individual builder areas. Osu, Central Accra, and Nima were selected to represent traditional housing areas. Surveys of households within districts were purely on a random basis, and the survey targeted conventional dwellings (houses, apartments, and compounds) and did not include informal structures (slums, kiosks, etc.). A target of thirty heads of households was established for each urban locality. The focus on heads of households is justified because prior research has demonstrated that housing costs are the sole responsibility of the head of household (Tipple et al. 1999, 280). In all, 300 heads of households were sampled and surveyed.

I supplemented the household data by examining the newly established real estate sector by reviewing advertisements in newspapers, Web sites, international magazines, and promotional literature produced by real estate companies. I analyzed all real estate advertisements in three leading national newspapers—*Daily Graphic,* the *Mirror,* and the *Ghanaian Times*—from 1983 to 2003. These newspapers not only accounted for the largest national circulation figures, but real estate agents rate the listings in them as the premier national property listings. The advertisements allowed me to identify property developers involved in building gated communities. I identified sixteen companies and twenty-three projects, and contacted these developers for brochures, house prices, and links to Web sites.

Third, my research draws on four locally produced data sets. Data on foreign companies was provided to me by the GIPC, which is the organization that oversees all foreign direct investment into the country. By law, all companies are required to register with the GIPC. It assembles data on a quarterly basis and provided me with a listing of all companies, investments, and locations of projects by sector, by partnership arrangement (wholly foreign-owned, JV etc.), and dollar amount for 1994 through 2004.

In addition, the Bank of Ghana provided me with data on remittances. The Bank of Ghana is the country's central bank. As part of financial liberalization efforts, the bank in 1990 introduced mandatory reporting procedures, whereby all financial institutions must report on a monthly basis the value of foreign inward transfers. The bank assembles data that measure the dollar value of private transfers, with a breakdown by geographical origins and financial institution (banks and nonbanks that operate money transfer schemes) for the source of the transfers. Because of the sensitivity of the information, data were made available to me at the aggregate level for 1994 through 2003.

The GSS also provided me with the 2000 population and housing census results for Greater Accra. Although the complete 2000 housing and population census has not been officially published, it is available to the research community and portions of the results were released for the purposes of this research. This data was used to assess changes in dwelling units as well as the spatial organization of the residential environment.

Additional data was collected from numerous interviews undertaken with key informants (e.g., local academics, researchers, journalists, representatives from international organizations (e.g., COHRE, UN-Habitat), private developers, real estate agents, property developers, residential associations, new property owners, return migrants, national ministries (e.g., Ministry of Works and Housing, Town and Country Planning Department), local government officials (e.g., AMA, Ashiedu Keteke Sub-Metro), GREDA, property management companies, bank officials, foreign companies, nongovernmental organizations (e.g., People's Dialogue on Human Settlements (PD) and Land for Life), community organizations (e.g., Ghana Homeless Peoples Federation [GHPF], the GaDangme Organization), and a nonprofit organization (Centre for Public Interest Law [CEPIL]). Group as well as individual interviews were held with Old Fadama and Agbogbloshie residents, upper-income residents in gated communities, and returnee migrants in East Airport, Osu, and Labadi. I also attended weekly meeting of various savings groups in Old Fadama to assess how their organization works from the ground upward. The sources and dates of many of these interviews are footnoted in the text.

# Works Cited

Accra Metropolitan Assembly (AMA). 1999. *Five-Year Medium Term Development Plan*. Report. Accra: AMA.

Accra Metropolitan Assembly (AMA) and Ministry of Works and Housing. 2002. *A Strategic Action Plan to Address the Issue of Squatter/Temporary Developments in the Metropolis*. Accra: AMA.

Accra Planning and Development Programme, UNDP, and Habitat. 1992. *Strategic Plan for the Greater Accra Metropolitan Area*. Accra: UNDP and Habitat.

Accra Studio. 2003. http://www.arch.columbia.edu/Studio/Spring2003/UP/Accra/index.html.

ACP Estates. 2004. *A Quality Lifestyle*. Report. Accra: ACP Estates.

Acquah, Ione. 1957. *Accra Survey*. London: Univ. of London Press.

Addison, E. K. Y. 2004. *The Macroeconomic Impact of Remittances*. Report. Accra: Bank of Ghana.

Africa Online. 2001. "Ghana: Security Firms Want Arms—Crooks Join the Industry." http://www. Africa.online.com/site/articles/1,3,3062.jsp.

Agbosu, Lennox Kwame. 2003. *Problems of Land Transactions in Ghana*. Paper presented at the Roundtable on Land Administration Reform in Ghana. Accra, Ghana, Apr. 4–7.

Agyepong, Kofi. 2006. "Opportunity International Makes Head Way." *Accra Daily Mail* July 5. http://www.accra-mail.com/mailnews. asp?ID=17183.

Ammassari, Savina. 2004. "From Nation-building to Entrepreneurship: The Impact of Elite Return Migrants in Cote D'Ivoire and Ghana." *Population, Space and Place* 10: 133–54.

———. 2005. "The Development Impact of Returning Migrants." *Cooperation South* 13: 81–101.

Anarfi, John, Stephen Kwankye, Ababio Ofuso-Mensah, and Richmond Tiemoko. 2003. *Migration to and from Ghana: A Background Paper*. Development

Research Center on Migration, Globalization and Poverty, Working Paper No. 4. Univ. of Sussex, UK.

Andersen, Jorgen, Jorgen Andreasen, and Graham Tipple. 2006. "The Demise of Compound Houses: Consequences for the Low Income Population of Kumasi, Ghana." *RICS Research Paper Series* 6: 1–35.

Antwi, Adarkwah, and John Adams. 2003a. "Economic Rationality and Informal Urban Land Transactions in Accra, Ghana." *Journal of Property Research* 20: 67–90.

———. 2003b. "Rent-seeking Behavior and Its Economic Costs in Urban Land Transactions in Accra, Ghana." *Urban Studies* 40: 2083–98.

Appadurai, Arjun. 2000. "Grassroots Globalization and the Research Imagination: Anxieties of the Global." *Public Culture* 12: 1–19.

———. 2001. "Deep Democracy: Urban Governmentality and the Horizon of Politics." *Environment and Urbanization* 2: 23–43.

Appiahene-Gyamfi, Joseph. 2003. "Urban Crime Trends and Patterns in Ghana: the Case of Accra." *Journal of Criminal Justice* 31: 13–23.

Arhinful, Daniel Kojo. 2001. *We Think of Them—How Ghanaian Migrants in Amsterdam Assist Relatives at Home.* African Studies Center (ASC), Research Report No. 62. Univ. of Leiden.

Armstrong, Warwick, and Terence McGee. 1986. *Theatres of Accumulation: Studies in Asian and Latin American Urbanization.* New York: Routledge Kegan & Paul.

Asiedu, Alex. 2003. *Some Benefits of Migrants Return Visits to Ghana.* International Workshop on Migration and Poverty in West Africa. Univ. of Sussex, UK, Mar. 13–14.

Atkinson, Rowland, and Sarah Blandy. 2006. *Gated Communities.* New York: Routledge.

Bank of Ghana. 2004. *The Macroeconomic Impact of Remittances in Ghana.* Report. Accra: Bank of Ghana Research Office.

Barr, Abigail M. 1995. *The Missing Factor: Entrepreneurial Networks, Enterprises and Economic Growth in Ghana.* Centre for the Study of African Economies, Working Paper: 95–111. Univ. of Oxford, UK.

Beaverstock, John, Phil Hubbard, and John Rennie Short. 2004. "Getting Away with It? Exposing the Geographies of the Super-Rich." *Geoforum* 35: 401–7.

Bebbington, Anthony. 2004. "NGOs and Uneven Development: Geographies of Development Intervention." *Progress in Human Geography* 28: 725–45.

Berger, Joseph. 2002. "American Dream Is a Ghanaian Home." *New York Times,* Aug. 21, B1, B6.

Berkhout, A. Bram, Michael Brink, and Evelyn Hello. 2005. *Return Migration and Employment: The Possibilities for Support Investigated.* Regioplan, Policy Research No. 1158. Amsterdam: The Netherlands Migration Institute and the Dutch Interchurch Organization for Development and Cooperation.

Berry, Sara. 2000. *Chiefs Know Their Boundaries: Essays on Property, Power and the Past in Asante, 1896–1996.* Portsmouth, N.H.: Heinemann.

Black, Richard, Russell King, and Julie Litchfield. 2003. *Transnational Migration, Return and Development in West Africa.* Sussex Centre for Migration Research, Final Research Report. Univ. of Sussex.

Black, Richard, Russell King, and Richmond Tiemoko. 2003. *Migration, Return and Small Enterprise Development in Ghana: A Route out of Poverty?* International Workshop on Migration and Poverty in West Africa. Univ. of Sussex, UK, Mar. 13–14.

Blakely, Edward James, and Mary Gail Snyder. 1997. *Fortress America: Gated Communities in the United States.* Washington D.C.: Brookings Institution Press.

Boadi, Owusu Kwasi, and Marku Kuitunen. 2002. "Urban Waste Pollution in the Korle Lagoon, Accra, Ghana." *The Environmentalist* 22: 301–9.

Bowditch, Nathaniel. 1999. *The Last Emerging Market. From Asian Tigers to African Lions? The Ghana File.* Westport: Praeger.

Brah, Avtar. 1996. *Cartographies of Diasporas: Contesting Identities.* London: Routledge.

Brand, Richard. 1972a. "A Geographical Interpretation of the European Influence on Accra, Ghana since 1877." Ph.D. diss., Columbia Univ.

———. 1972b. "The Spatial Organization of Residential Areas in Accra, Ghana, with Particular Reference to Aspects of Modernization." *Economic Geography* 48: 284–98.

Bump, Micah. 2006. "Ghana: Searching for Opportunities at Home and Abroad." http://www.migrationinformation.org/Profiles/display.cfm?id=381

Caglar, Ayse. 2006. "Hometown Associations, the Rescaling of State Spatiality and Migrant Grassroots Transnationalism." *Global Networks* 6: 1–22.

Campbell, John. 1994. "Urbanization, Culture and the Politics of Urban Development in Ghana, 1875–1980." *Urban Anthropology* 23: 409–50.

Centre on Housing Rights and Evictions (COHRE). 2004. *A Precarious Future: the Informal Settlement of Agbogbloshie Accra, Ghana.* Unpublished report.

Coates, Ta-Neshie. 2006. "Ghana's New Money." *Time.* http://www.time.com/globalbusines/ptintout/0,8816,1229122,00.html.

Cohen, Jeffrey. 2005. "Remittance Outcomes and Migration: Theoretical Contests, Real Opportunities." *Studies in Comparative International Development* 40: 88–112.

Coy, Martin, and Martin Pohler. 2002. "Gated Communities in Latin American Megacities: Case Studies in Brazil and Argentina." *Environment and Planning B* 29: 355–70.

Czaja, Ronald, and Johnny Blair. 2004. *Designing Surveys: A Guide to Decisions and Procedures.* 2d Edition. Thousand Oaks, Calif.: Pine Forge Press.

*Daily Graphic.* 2002a. "Another Sodom and Gomorrah in the Making." Dec. 12, 16–17.

———. 2002b. "Dusk-to-Dawn Curfew in North Following Chief's Beheading." Mar. 28, 1.

———. 2002c. "Public and Vested Lands to Be Offered on the Open Market." Sept. 12, 1.

———. 2002d. "Advertiser's Announcement. Statement on GaDangme Lands." June 28, 4.

———. 2003. "Accra Is Now Safe." Feb. 27, 1.

———. 2006. "Taxing Remittances." Mar. 21, 1.

Davis, Mike. 2006. *Planet of Slums.* New York: Verso.

D'Cruz, Celine, and Diane Mitlin. 2004. *Shack/Slum Dwellers International: One Experience of the Contribution of Membership Organization to Pro-poor Urban Development.* Paper. London: International Institute for Environment and Development.

DeFillippis, James. 2004. *Unmaking Goliath: Community Control in the Face of Global Capital.* New York: Routledge.

De Soto, Hernando. 2000. *The Mystery of Capital: Why Capitalism Triumphs in the West and Fails Everywhere Else.* New York: Basic Books.

Diko, Johnson, and Graham Tipple. 1992. "Migrants Build at Home: Long Distance Housing Development by Ghanaians in London." *Cities* 9: 288–94.

Dillman, Don. 1978. *Mail and Telephone Surveys: The Total Design Method.* New York: Wiley.

Donaldson, Ronnie, and Marais Lochner 2002. *Transforming Rural and Urban Spaces in South Africa During the 1990s: Reform, Restitution, Restructuring.* Pretoria: Africa Institute of South Africa.

Dzorgbo, Dan-Bright. 1998. *Ghana in Search of Development.* Uppsala: Uppsala Univ.

*Economist.* 2001. "Globalisation and its Critics. A Survey of Globalisation." Sept. 27. http://economist.com/surveys/displayStory.cfm?story_id=795995

———. 2002. "Outward Bound." Sept. 26, 38–40.

*Financial Times.* 1999. "Ghana Survey" Nov. 4, 3.

FIT. 1999. *FIT Business Directory.* Accra: FIT.

———. 2003. *FIT Business Directory.* Accra: FIT.

GaDangme Council. 1999. *Burning Issues on GaDangme Lands.* Accra: GaDangme Council.

———. 2002. *A Mid-Term Briefing on the Challenges, Acts and Accomplishments of the GaDangme Council.* Accra: GaDangme Council.

Garlick, Peter. 1960. "Levantine Trading Firms in Ghana." *Economic Bulletin of Ghana* 4: 1–12.

Garreau, Joel. 1991. *Edge City: Life on the New Frontier.* New York: Anchor Books.

*Ghanaian Chronicle.* 2001. "Demolish Sodom and Gomorrah." Mar. 29, 2.

———. 2004. "Shocking Revelation: Only 5% of Ghanaians Have Bank Accounts." Aug 30, 1.

Ghana Cyber Group. 2006. "The Ghana Technology Park: a Ground Breaking Business and Innovation Centre." http://www.ghanacybergroup.com/business/techpark.asp.?mc=gtp.

Ghana Estates. 2004. http://www.ghanaestates.com/info/news/smpl-nyork.php.

Ghana Homes Incorporated (GHI). 2004. http://www.myghanahome.com.

*Ghanaian Times.* 1983–2003. Accra: New Times Corporation.

Ghana Investment Promotion Centre (GIPC). 2004a. *Ghana Investment Profile: Property Development.* Accra: GIPC.

———. 2004b. http://www.gipc.org.gh/documents/WEBRPT4Q03.htm.

———. 2006. *Statistics on Registered Projects.* Accra: GIPC.

———. 2007. *Statistics on Registered Projects.* Accra: GIPC.

Ghana Police Headquarters. 1980–2001. *Official Crime Data.* Accra: Ghana Police Service, Criminal Data Services Bureau.

*Ghana Real Estates Magazine International.* 2004a. Regalon International, 65.

———. 2004b. "Ghana's Underdeveloped Construction Industry Dominated by Foreign Construction Firms." *Ghana Real Estates Magazine* 1: 12.

*Ghana Review.* 2001. http://www.ghanareview.com/Homecoming%20-%20KOA.html.

Ghana Statistical Services (GSS). 2002. *2000 Population and Housing Census: Special Report on Urban Localities.* Accra: GSS.

———. 2003. *Ghana Living Standards Survey, 1998–1999.* Accra: GSS.

———. 2004. *2000 Population and Housing Census*. Unpublished data. Accra: GSS.

Ghanaweb. 2006a. *Remittances Policy That Works: The Case Of Ghana*. http://www
.ghanaweb.com/GhanaHomePage/NewsArchive/artikel.php?ID=106354.

———. 2006b. http://www.ghanaweb.com/GhanaHomePage/NewsArchive/
artikel .php?ID=96936.

Gifford, Paul. 2004. *Ghana's New Christianity: Pentecostalism in a Globalizing African Economy*. Bloomington: Indiana Univ. Press.

Gough, Katherine, and Paul Yankson. 1997. *Continuity and Change in Peri-urban
Accra*. Copenhagen: Danish Council for Development Research.

Government of Ghana (GOG). 1961. *Ghana Land and Concessions: Bulletin no.
132960*. Legal document. Ghana Land Registry.

Graham, Stephan, and Simon Marvin. 2001. *Splintering Urbanism: Networked
Infrastructures, Technological Mobilities and the Urban Condition*. New York:
Routledge.

Grant, Richard. 1999. "Foreign Company Survey." Syracuse University.

———. 2001. "Liberalisation Policies and Foreign Companies in Accra, Ghana."
*Environment and Planning A* 33: 997–1014.

———. 2004. Field Survey.

———. 2005. "The Emergence of Gated Communities in a West African Context."
*Urban Geography* 26: 661–83.

Grant, Richard, and Jan Nijman. 2002. "Globalization and the Corporate Geography of Cities in the Less-Developed World." *Annals of the Association of American Geographies* 92: 320–40.

———. 2004. "The Re-scaling of Uneven Development in Ghana and India." *Tijd-
schrift voor Economishe en Sociale Geografie* (Journal of Economic and Social
Geography) 95: 467–81.

Grant, Richard, and John Rennie Short, eds. 2002. *Globalization and the Margins*.
London: Macmillan/Palgrave.

Grant, Richard, and Paul Yankson. 2003. "Accra: City Profile." *Cities* 20: 65–74.

Grayson, Leslie. 1979. *Managing the Economic Development of Ghana*. Charlottes-
ville: Univ. of Virginia.

Gri Newsreel. 2003. "AMA Dialogue with Sodom and Gomorrah Squatters." Jul.
18, 1.

Gugler, Josef. 2004. *World Cities Beyond the West. Globalization, Development, and
Inequality*. New York: Cambridge University Press.

Gugler, Josef, and William G. Flanagan. 1978. *Urbanization and Social Change in
West Africa*. New York: Cambridge Univ. Press.

Gymiah-Boadi, E., and Richard Asante 2003. *Minorities in Ghana*. Report prepared for the UN High Commissioner on Human Rights, Sub-Commission on Promotion and Protection of Human Rights Working Group on Minorities, Ninth Session, May 12–16, New York.

HABITAT (United Nations Center for Human Settlements). 2001. *Cities in a Globalizing World: Global Report on Human Settlements 2001*. Sterling: Earthscan.

Hale, Briony. 2003. "In Search of Africa's Silicon Valley." http://news.bbc.co.uk/2/hi/business/3000004.stm.

Hammond, Nikoi. 2006. "The Social Costs of Real Estate Market Information Gaps in Ghana." *Urban Policy and Research* 14: 391–408.

Hannerz, Ulf. 1996. *Transnational Connection: Culture, People, Places*. London: Routledge.

Hansen, Karen, and Mariken Vaa, eds. 2004. *Reconsidering Informality: Perspectives from Urban Africa*. Stockholm: Nordiska Afrikainstitutet.

Hanson, Kobena. 2004. "Rethinking the Akan Household: Acknowledging the Importance of Culturally and Linguistically Meaningful Images." *Africa Today* 51: 27–45.

———. 2005. "Landscapes of Survival and Escape: Social Networking and Urban Livelihoods in Ghana." *Environment and Planning A* 37: 1291–1310.

Harrison, Phillip. 2006. "On the Edge of Reason: Planning and Urban Fortunes in Africa." *Urban Studies* 43: 319–35.

Henry, Leroy, and Giles Mohan. 2003. "Making Homes: The Ghanaian Diaspora, Institutions and Development." *Journal of International Development* 15: 611–22.

Higazi, Adam. 2005. *Ghana Country Study: A Report on Informal Remittance Systems in African, Caribbean and Pacific Countries*. ERSC Center on Migration, Policy and Society Working Paper 8. University of Oxford.

Hubbard, James. 1925. *Accra: A Geographical Study of the Historical Background to Development Up to 1920*. Accra: Gold Coast Government Printer.

Huchzermeyer, Marie. 2001. "Consent and Contradiction: Scholarly Responses to the Capital Subsidy Model for Informal Settlement Intervention in South Africa." *Urban Forum* 12: 71–106.

———. 2004. *Unlawful Occupation: Informal Settlements and Urban Policy in South Africa and Brazil*. Trenton: Africa World Press.

Interpol. 2004. www.interpol.int/public/statistics/ics/default.asp.

Jack, Malcolm, and Farouk Braimah. 2004. *Feasibility Study for the Application of Community-led Infrastructure Finance Facility (CLIFF) Operations in Ghana*. Homeless International Unpublished Paper: 1–60.

Jackson, Peter, Philip Crang, and Claire Dwyer. 2004. *Transnational Spaces*. New York: Routledge.

Jones, Gavin, ed. 2003. *Urban Land Markets in Transition*. Boston: Lincoln Land Institute.

Juul, Kristine, and Christina Lund, eds. 2002. *Negotiating Property in Africa*. Portsmouth, N.H.: Heinemann.

Kabki, Mirjam, Valentina Mazzucato, and Ernest Appiah. 2004. "'Wo bebane a eye bebree': The Economic Impact of Remittances of Netherlands-based Ghanaian Migrants on Rural Ashanti." *Population, Space and Place* 10: 85–97.

Kasanga Kasim, Jeff Cochrane, Russell King, and Michael Roth. 1996. *Land Markets and Legal Contradictions in the Peri-Urban Area of Accra Ghana: Informant Interviews and Secondary Data Investigations*. Land Tenure Research Center, Working Paper No 127. Madison: Univ. of Wisconsin–Madison.

Kea, Richard. 1982. *Settlements, Trade, and Politics in the Seventeenth–Century Gold Coast*. Baltimore: The Johns Hopkins Univ. Press.

Kigotho, Wachira. 2004. "A 'Swarthmore' Grows in Ghana." *Chronicle of Higher Education* 51: A36.

Killick, Tony. 1978. *Development Economics in Action: A Study of Economic Policies in Ghana*. New York: St. Martin's Press.

King, Anthony. 1995. *The Bungalow: The Production of Global Culture*. New York: Oxford University Press.

———. 2004. *Spaces of Global Culture*. New York: Routledge.

King, Anthony, and Abidin Kusno. 2000. "On Be(ij)ing in the World: Postmodernism, Globalization and the Making of Transnational Space in China." In *Postmodernism and China,* edited by Arif Dirlik and Xudong Zhang, 41–67. Durham, N.C.: Duke Univ. Press.

Knox, Paul, ed. 1993. *The Restless Urban Landscape*. Englewood Cliffs, N.J.: Prentice-Hall.

Konadu-Agyemang, Kwadwo. 1991. "Reflections on the Absence of Squatter Settlements in West African Cities: The Case of Kumasi, Ghana." *Urban Studies* 28: 139–51.

———. 2000. "The Best of Times and the Worst of Times: Structural Adjustment Programs and Uneven Development in Africa: The Case of Ghana." *Professional Geographer* 52: 469–83.

———. 2001a. "A Survey of Housing Conditions and Characteristics in Accra, an African City." *Habitat International* 25: 15–33.

———. 2001b. *The Political Economy of Housing and Urban Development in Africa: Ghana's Experience from Colonial Times to 1998.* Westport: Praeger.

Korboe, David. 1992. "Family-Houses in Ghanaian Cities: To Be or Not to Be?" *Urban Studies* 29: 1159–72.

Landman, Karina. 2004. *Gated Communities in South Africa.* Paper presented at the Institute for Security Studies, Pretoria, South Africa.

Levitt, Peggy. 2001. *The Transnational Villagers.* Los Angeles: Univ. of California Press.

Levitt, Peggy, and Nina Glick Schiller. 2004. "Conceptualizing Simultaneity: A Transnational Social Field Perspective on Society." *International Migration Review* 38: 1002–39.

Mabin, Alan. 2001. "Contested Urban Futures—Report on a Global Gathering in Johannesburg, 2000." *International Journal of Urban and Regional Research* 25: 180–84.

Mabogunje, Akin. 1992. *Perspectives on Urban Land and Urban Management Policies in Sub-Saharan Africa.* World Bank Technical Paper No. 196. Washington, D.C.: World Bank.

MacDonald, George. 1898. *The Gold Coast, Past and Present: A Short Description of the Country and Its People.* London: Longmans.

Machan, Dyan. 2005: "Opportunities Never End: While the West Gets Beneficent Again Toward Africa, Some in the Emblematic Nation of Ghana Stress Other Priorities." *Forbes.* http://www.forbes.com/global/2005/0606/026_print.html.

Maloney, Conor. 2004. "Private Housing Estate Development and the Restructuring of Residential Geography in Accra." M.A. thesis, London School of Economics.

Malpezzi, Stephen, and Stephen Mayo. 1997. "The Demand for Housing in Developing Countries." *Economic Development and Cultural Change* 35: 687–721.

Manet. 2004. *Your Innovative Housing Provider.* Report. Accra: Manet.

Mazzucato, Valentina. 2005. "Ghanaian Migrant's Double Engagement: A Transnational View of Development and Integration Policies." *Global Migration Perspectives* 48: 1–18.

Mazzucato, Valentina, Mirjam Kabki, and Lothar Smith. 2006. "Transnational Migration and the Economy of Funerals: Changing Practices in Ghana." *Development and Change* 37: 1047–72.

Mends, Theodora. 2006. *Property Valuation in Ghana: Constraints and Contradictions.* Paper presented at the Promoting Land Administration and Good Governance Conference, Accra, Ghana, March 8–11.

Miller, Darlene. 2007. "Changing African Cityscapes: Regional Claims of African Labor at South African-owned Shopping Malls." In *Cities in Contemporary Africa,* edited by Martin Murray and Garth Myers, 149–72. New York: Palgrave/Macmillan.

Ministry of Local Government, Government of Ghana. 1990. *Housing Needs Assessment Study Final Report.* Report. Kumasi: Housing and Urban Development Associates.

Mirror. 1983–2003. *Property Advertisements.* Accra: The Mirror Newspaper.

Mitlin, Diane, and David Satterthwaite, eds. 2004. *Empowering Squatter Citizens: Local Government, Civil Society and Poverty Reduction.* Sterling: Earthscan.

Mmieh, Frederick, and Nana Owusu-Frimpong. 2004. "State Policies and the Challenges in Attracting Foreign Direct Investment: A Review of the Ghana Experience." *Thunderbird International Business Review* 46: 575–99.

Mohan, Giles. 2006. "Embedded Cosmopolitanism and the Politics of Obligation: The Ghanaian Diaspora and Development." *Environment and Planning A* 38: 867–83.

Mueller, Glenn, and Barry Ziering. 1992. "Real Estate Portfolio Diversification Using Economic Diversification." *Journal of Real Estate Research* 4: 375–86.

Murray, Martin. 2004. *The Evolving Spatial Form of Cities in a Globalizing Economy: Johannesburg and Sao Paulo.* Occasional Paper No. 5. Democracy and Governance Programme. Cape Town: Human Sciences Research Council.

Murray, Martin, and Garth Myers. 2007. *Cities in Contemporary Africa.* New York: Palgrave/Macmillan.

Myers, Garth. 2003. *Verandahs of Power: Colonialism and Space in Urban Africa.* Syracuse: Syracuse Univ. Press.

*News from Africa.* 2002. "End of the Road for 'Sodom and Gomorrah' Squatters." http://www.newsfromafrica.org/articles/art_827.html.

Odame-Larbi, W. 1996. "Spatial Planning and Urban Fragmentation in Accra." *Third World Planning Review* 18: 193–214.

Ofori, Sam. 2002. *Regional Policy and Regional Planning in Ghana.* Ashgate: Burlington.

Okonkwo, Uli. 1999. "Migrants and Housing Investments: Theory and Evidence from Nigeria." Ph.D. diss., Northwestern Univ., Evanston, Ill.

Oncu, Ayse, and Petra Weyland, eds. 1997. *Space, Culture and Power: New Identities in Globalizing Cities.* London: Zed Press.

Orozco, Manuel. 2005. *Diaspora, Development and Transnational Integration: Ghanaian in the U.S., U.K. and Germany.* Institute for the Study of International Migration and Inter-American Dialogue.

Osili, Una. 2004. "Migrants and Housing Investment: Theory and Evidence From Nigeria." *Economic Development and Cultural Change* 52: 821–42.

Pacione, Michael. 2005. *Urban Geography: A Global Perspective.* 2d Edition. New York: Routledge.

Parker, John. 2000. *Making the Town: Ga State and Society in Early Colonial Accra.* Portsmouth: Heinemann.

Peil, Margaret. 1976. "African Squatter Settlements: A Comparative Study." *Urban Studies* 13: 155–66.

Pellow, Deborah. 2002. *Landlords and Lodgers: Socio-Spatial Organization in an Accra Community.* Westport: Praeger.

———. 2003. "New Spaces in Accra: Transnational Houses." *City and Society* 15: 59–86.

Perlman, Janice. 1976. *The Myth of Marginality: Urban Poverty and Politics in Rio de Janeiro.* Berkeley: Univ. of California Press.

Portes, Alejandro, Luis Guarnid, and Patricia Landolt. 1999. "The Study of Transnationalism: Pitfalls and Promise of an Emergent Field." *Ethnic and Racial Studies* 22: 217–37.

Portes, Alejandro, William J. Haller, and Luis Eduardo Guarnizo. 2002. "Transnational Entrepreneurs: the Emergence and Determination of Immigrant Economic Adoption." *American Sociological Review* 67: 278–98.

Quarcoopome, Samuel. 1992. "Urbanization and Land Alienation and Politics in Accra." *Institute of African Studies Research Review* 8: 40–54.

Rakodi, Carole. 1997. "Residential Property Markets in African Cities." In *The Urban Challenge in Africa: Growth and Management of Its Largest Cities,* edited by Carole Rakodi, 371–410. Tokyo: United Nations Univ. Press.

———. Rakodi, Carole. 2004. *African Town and Cities: Powerhouses of Economic Development or Slums of Despair?* Paper presented at the Urban Futures Conference. Jul. 8–10, Chicago.

Ranney, David. 2003. *Global Decisions Local Collisions: Urban Life in the New World Order.* Philadelphia: Temple Univ. Press.

Regalon. 2004. *Property Developers.* Accra: Regalon.

Regimanuel Gray. 2004. *Your Complete Information on Owning a Regimanuel Gray Home.* Report. Accra: Regimanuel Gray.

Robins, Steven. 2004. "Grounding Globalization from Below: 'Global Citizens' in Local Spaces." Paper. Department of Anthropology and Sociology, Univ. of Western Cape, South Africa.

Robinson, Jennifer. 2006. *Ordinary Cities*. New York: Routledge.

Rogerson, Christian. 2005. "Toward the World-class African City: Planning Economic Development in Johannesburg." *Africa Insight* 34: 12–21.

Routledge, Paul. 2003. "Convergence Space: Process Geographies of Grassroots Globalization Networks." *Transactions of the Institute of British Geographers* 28: 333–49.

Royal Palms. 2004. www.myghana.home.com/homes/royalpalms/.

Scott, Allen. 2002. "Regional Push: Towards a Geography of Development and Growth in Low- and Middle-Income Countries." *Third World Quarterly* 23: 137–61.

Short, John Rennie. 2004a. "Black Holes and Loose Connection in the Global Urban Network." *Professional Geographer* 56: 295–302.

———. 2004b. *Global Metropolitan: Globalizing Cities in a Capitalist World*. New York: Routledge.

Simon, David. 1992a. "Urbanization, Globalization, and Economic Crises in Africa" In *The Urban Challenge in Africa: Growth and Management of Its Large Cities*, edited by Carole Rakodi, 74–118. Tokyo: United Nations Univ. Press.

———. 1992b. *Cities, Capital and Development: African Cities in the World Economy*. London: Belhaven Press.

Simone, AbouMaliq. 2004. *For the City Yet to Come: Changing African Life in Four Cities*. Durham, N.C.: Duke Univ. Press.

Smith, Lothar, and Valentina Mazzucato. 2003. *Houses, Businesses and Urban Livelihoods: The Influence of Transnational Networks on Economic Activities in Accra, Ghana*. Paper presented at the International Workshop on Migration and Poverty in West Africa, Univ. of Sussex, Mar. 13–14.

Songsore, Jacob. 2003. *Regional Development in Ghana: The Theory and Reality*. Accra: Woeli Publishing Services.

Stanley, Henry. 1874. *Coomassie and Magdala*. New York: Harper.

Taylor, Peter. 2001. "The New Geography of Civil Society: NGOs in the World-City Network." *GAWC Research Bulletin* No. 114.

———. 2005. "New Political Geographies: Global Civil Society and Global Governance Through World City Networks." *Political Geography* 24: 703–30.

Taysec. 2004. *Invest in a Taysec Home Today*. Report. Accra: Taysec.

Tiemoko, Richmond. 2004. "Migration, Return and Socio-economic Change in West Africa: The Role of the Family." *Population, Space and Place* 10: 155–74.

Tipple, Graham, and David Korboe. 1998. "Housing Policy in Ghana: Towards a Supply-oriented Future." *Habitat International* 22: 245–57.

Tipple, Graham, and Kenneth Willis. 1992. "Why Should Ghanaians Build Houses in Urban Areas? An Introduction to Private Sector Housing in Ghana." *Cities* 2: 60–74.

Tipple, Graham, David Korboe, and Guy Garrod. 1997. "A Comparison of Original Owners and Inheritors in Housing Supply and Extension in Kumasi, Ghana." *Environment and Planning B* 24: 889–902.

Tipple, Graham, David Korboe, Guy Garrod, and Kenneth Willis. 1999. "Housing Supply in Ghana: A Study of Accra, Kumasi and Berekum." *Progress in Planning* 51: 253–324.

Tostensen, Arne, Inge Tvedten, and Mariken Vaa. 2001. *Associational Life in African Cities: Popular Responses to the Urban Crisis.* Stockholm: Nordiska Afrikainstitutet.

Trasacco Valley. 2004. *Experience the Dream.* Report. Accra: Trasacco Valley.

Tuurosong, Damasus. 2004. "Real Estate: Scarcity in the Midst of a Boom." *Business Watch Online* 3: 1–5.

UN-Habitat. 2003. *The Challenge of Slums: Global Report on Human Settlements 2003.* London: Earthscan Publications.

———. 2005. *Forced Evictions—Towards Solutions? First Report of the Advisory Group on Forced Evictions to the Executive Director of UN-Habitat.* Pietermaritzburg: Interpak Books.

United Nations. 2003. *Investment Policy Review: Ghana.* New York: United Nations.

United Nations Conference on Trade and Development. 2002. *Ghana's Gateway Program.* http://r0.unctad.org/ttl/ppt-2002-11-25/ghana/ghana-present.htm.

United Nations Development Programme and HABITAT. 1992. *Strategic Plan for Greater Accra Metropolitan Area (GAMA)* 3 vols. Accra: UNDP and HABITAT.

United Nations Human Settlement Programme. 2003. *The Challenge of the Slums: Global Report on Human Settlements 2003.* London: Earthscan Publications.

United Nations Industrial Development Organization. 2003. *Project Profiles: Ghana.* Vienna: UNIDO.

Van der Merwe, Hannes. 2004. "The Global Cities of Sub-Saharan African: Fact or Fiction?" *Urban Forum* 14: 320–46.

Waldinger, Roger and Fitzgerald, David. 2004. "Transnationalism in Question." *American Journal of Sociology* 109: 1177–195.

Webster, Chris, Georg Glasze, and Klaus Frantz. 2002. "The Global Spread of Gated Communities." *Environment and Planning B.* 29: 315–20.

World Bank. 1994. *Adjustment in Africa: Reforms, Results and the Road Ahead.* New York: Oxford Univ. Press.

———. 2005. *African Development Indicators.* Washington D.C.: The World Bank.

Wu, Fulung. 2002. "Sociospatial Differentiation in Urban China: Evidence from Shanghai's Real Estate Markets." *Environment and Planning A* 34: 1591–1615.

Yeboah, Ian. 2001. "Structural Adjustment and Emerging Urban Form in Accra, Ghana." *Africa Today* 7: 61–89.

———. 2003a. "Demographic and Housing Aspects of Structural Adjustment and Emerging Urban Form in Accra, Ghana." *Africa Today* 10: 106–119.

———. 2003b. *GaDangme, Urban Poverty and the Emergence of the Underclass.* Paper presented at the Annual Meeting of the African Studies Association, Boston, Oct. 30–Nov. 2.

Zachary, Pascal. 2005. "Diaspora Capitalism and Exile as a Way of Life. Some Observations on the Political and Economic Mobilization of Dispersed Peoples." http://www.nautilus.org/ archives/virtual-diasporas/paper/Zachary.html.

# Index

Italic page numbers denote figures, maps, and tables.